Contents

Miriam B. Loo's
MEAL-IN-ONE FAVORITES

Recipes Compiled by Miriam B. Loo

Illustrated by Marsha K. Howe

Photography by Ron Oatney

Dear Friends,

Although one often thinks of a one-dish meal as being a casserole, there are actually many other types of dishes that serve the same "meal-in-one" function. There are soups, chowders, stews, gumbos, quiches, crepes, pizzas, stir-fries, whole meal salads, and sandwiches. And a meat or meats cooked in a roaster or Dutch oven with vegetables make a hearty meal as well.

Meal-in-one dishes are a real boon to homemakers because they can be made in double quantities to feed a crowd or to divide so half can be frozen. Most can be prepared in the morning or the day before and baked or heated just before serving. Most are easy on the budget, too.

Naturally you might want to serve a meal-in-one dish with some kind of accompaniment, but these can be quick and easy side dishes such as a bread, a tossed salad, a fruit, or a light dessert. Following most recipes in the book I have given you a suggestion for the accompaniment.

Good Eating!

Miriam B. Loo

Miriam B. Loo

Soups, Chowders, Stews, and Gumbos

Italian Stew with Meatballs

Meatballs:

1½ pounds lean ground beef
¾ cup cracker crumbs
2 eggs, beaten
2 tablespoons milk
¾ cup minced onion
¾ teaspoon dried Italian herb
   seasoning, crushed
¾ teaspoon salt
½ teaspoon freshly ground pepper
3 tablespoons vegetable oil

Combine ground beef, cracker crumbs, eggs, milk, onion, herb seasoning, salt, and pepper. Form into about 30 walnut-size meatballs. In large skillet, brown meatballs in vegetable oil over medium-high heat. Drain and set aside.

Stew:

¼ cup olive oil
¼ cup whole wheat flour
1 46-ounce can tomato-vegetable juice
1¼ pounds zucchini, sliced ¼-inch
   thick
1 medium onion, diced
1 green pepper, diced
½ pound fresh mushrooms, thinly
   sliced
1 small head cauliflower, cut into bite-
   size pieces
1 4-ounce can diced green chilies
2 teaspoons dried basil, crushed
1 teaspoon dried thyme, crushed
1 teaspoon salt
Several drops hot pepper sauce
Grated sharp Cheddar cheese

Heat olive oil in large pot. Add flour; cook and stir for 3 minutes. Add tomato-vegetable juice and continue to stir until well blended. Add zucchini, onion, pepper, mushrooms, and cauliflower; bring to boil, reduce heat, and simmer for 20 minutes or until vegetables are crisp-tender. Stir in chilies, seasonings, and hot pepper sauce; add meatballs. Cook for 10 minutes, stirring carefully several times. Top each serving with a spoonful of cheese.

Serves 8

Comment: Hot and zesty! A wedge of nicely browned corn bread would be a great addition.

Cover: Chicken-Shrimp Paella, see page 48.

Left, clockwise from the top: Chicken Gumbo with Rice, see page 8; Ham and Corn Chowder, see page 9; German Pea Soup, see page 6; Scotch Broth, see page 11.

German Pea Soup

2 cups dried split peas, soaked overnight and drained
5 cups water
4 cups chicken broth
2 onions, coarsely chopped
2 large carrots, coarsely grated
3 ribs celery, thinly sliced
2 cloves garlic, minced
½ bay leaf
1½ pounds ham hocks, sliced
Salt and freshly ground pepper to taste
3 knockwurst, sliced ½-inch thick (about 12 ounces)

Garnish:
½ cup dairy sour cream

Serves 8

In large kettle combine split peas, water, chicken broth, onions, carrots, celery, garlic, bay leaf, and ham hocks. Sprinkle lightly with salt and pepper; bring to boil, cover, and turn heat down to simmer. Cook for 1½ to 2 hours. Remove ham hocks and cut meat from bones into fine strips. Remove bay leaf and discard. Return ham to kettle; add knockwurst, bring to simmer, and cook for 5 minutes. If the soup is too thin, remove cover and boil for 5 minutes. Garnish each serving with a dollop of sour cream.

Comment: Apple muffins make a tasty contrast to the soup.

Turkey Chowder

1 pound uncooked ground turkey
½ cup cracker crumbs
2 tablespoons all-purpose flour
1 teaspoon salt
⅛ teaspoon freshly ground pepper
2 eggs
⅓ cup milk
2 tablespoons grated onion
8 cups turkey or chicken broth
4 medium carrots, sliced
3 medium new potatoes, pared and diced
½ cup water
¼ cup all-purpose flour
2 tablespoons fresh lemon juice

Garnish:
2 tablespoons chopped fresh parsley

Serves 8 to 10

Combine turkey, cracker crumbs, 2 tablespoons flour, salt, pepper, eggs, milk, and onion. Shape into 36 walnut-size meatballs. In large kettle, bring broth to boil. Add meatballs and return to boil; cover, reduce heat, and simmer 10 minutes. Remove meatballs from broth and set aside. Add carrots and potatoes to broth; cook for 20 minutes. Blend water and ¼ cup flour; add to broth, mix well, and cook 10 minutes. Add lemon juice and meatballs; cook until heated through.

Comment: Rich in flavor ... use leftover turkey bones to make your broth. Serve with brown bread and butter.

German Oxtail Stew

4 tablespoons vegetable oil
4 pounds oxtail, cut into 2-inch lengths
2 quarts water
1 large onion, chopped
2 cups diced carrot
1 cup diced turnip
1 cup diced celery
1 bay leaf
½ teaspoon dried thyme, crushed
4 to 5 whole peppercorns
1½ teaspoons salt or to taste
¾ cup pearl barley
1 cup diced potatoes
½ pound fresh mushrooms, sliced
Salt and freshly ground pepper to taste
Paprika

In large, heavy kettle heat 1 tablespoon vegetable oil; add oxtail pieces and brown well. Add water and bring to boil; skim for 15 minutes as residue rises to surface. Meanwhile, heat 2 tablespoons oil in large skillet; lightly brown onion, carrots, turnip, and celery. Add to soup kettle after the 15 minutes of skimming is completed. Bring to boil; add bay leaf, thyme, peppercorns, and salt; cover and simmer for 2 hours. Remove oxtail pieces; chill broth. Trim meat off bone and discard bones. Skim fat off broth, return meat to kettle, add barley, and bring to boil. Meanwhile, heat remaining 1 tablespoon oil in skillet and sauté potatoes and mushrooms over high heat, stirring, for 5 minutes. Add to kettle, bring to boil, and simmer for 40 to 45 minutes or until barley is tender. Remove from heat and correct seasoning with salt and pepper. Add a dash of paprika to each serving.

Makes 2 quarts

Comment: A big tureen of this hearty stew will go well with fresh scallions, celery sticks, slices of sharp Cheddar cheese, and hot pita bread.

Chicken Gumbo with Rice

2 tablespoons butter or margarine
1 small onion, minced
1 green pepper, chopped
1 sprig fresh thyme or parsley, minced
4 pounds frying chicken pieces
1 pound ham, diced
Salt and freshly ground pepper to taste
1 16-ounce can tomatoes, chopped
  (reserve juice)
4 ounces frozen sliced okra
1 bay leaf
1 quart chicken broth
4 cups hot cooked rice

Heat butter or margarine in large kettle; add onion, green pepper, and thyme or parsley; sauté until vegetables are limp. Add chicken and ham, sprinkle with salt and pepper, cover tightly, and simmer for 10 minutes. Add tomatoes with juice, okra, bay leaf, and chicken broth. Bring to boil; reduce heat and simmer over low heat for 2 hours, partially covered. Skim fat and discard. Taste for seasoning; add salt and pepper to taste. Serve from soup tureen into soup bowls over a generous portion of rice.

Serves 6

Comment: Try this southern favorite with hot buttered corn sticks.

Tuna-Shrimp Chowder

2 tablespoons butter or margarine
½ cup chopped onion
½ cup sliced celery
5 cups pared diced potatoes
2 cups sliced carrots
2 cups water
1 7-ounce can tuna, drained and flaked
1 4½-ounce can tiny shrimp, drained
1 pint fresh oysters (optional)
4 cups half-and-half
1 teaspoon salt
¼ teaspoon ground white pepper or to taste
Minced fresh dill or fresh parsley

In large kettle, melt butter or margarine; add onion and celery and sauté for 10 minutes. Add potatoes, carrots, and water; bring to boil. Lower heat, cover, and simmer 30 minutes, stirring occasionally, until carrots and potatoes are tender. Add tuna, shrimp, optional oysters (if large, cut in 3 pieces), and half-and-half; heat through. Stir in salt and pepper to taste. Serve in heated soup bowls with a sprinkling of dill or parsley.

Note: If only dried dill is available, sprinkle over chowder to taste.

Serves 8

Comment: A nice light taste of the sea. Serve with a big basket of warm oyster crackers.

Ham and Corn Chowder

8 slices bacon, cut into 1-inch pieces
1 cup sliced celery
½ cup sliced green pepper
1 onion, quartered and thinly sliced
1 clove garlic, minced
3 medium potatoes, diced
3 cups chicken broth
4 cups whole kernel corn, fresh or frozen
4 cups milk
2 cups cubed ham
⅛ teaspoon hot pepper sauce
1 teaspoon salt or to taste
Freshly ground pepper to taste
1 tablespoon minced fresh parsley
2 tablespoons real butter

Garnish:
Reserved bacon pieces
2 tablespoons minced fresh parsley

In large saucepan sauté bacon until nearly crisp. Remove and drain on paper towels; reserve. Remove all but 4 tablespoons drippings from saucepan; add celery, green pepper, onion, and garlic. Stir-fry for 5 minutes. Add potatoes and broth; simmer, covered, for 10 minutes. Purée 2 cups corn with ½ cup milk in blender; add puréed corn, remaining corn, and ham to the potatoes and broth; simmer for 10 minutes. Stir in remaining milk, hot pepper sauce, salt, pepper, and 1 tablespoon parsley; heat to just under boiling. Remove from heat and add butter. Garnish just before serving with reserved bacon pieces and 2 tablespoons parsley.

Serves 8 to 10

Comment: As an accompaniment, try toasted, buttered crackers with red currant jelly followed by warm apple pie with a wedge of Cheddar cheese.

Plymouth Succotash Stew

¼ pound salt pork, cubed
1½ pounds corned beef
1½ quarts water
2 pounds chicken pieces
2 15-ounce cans Great Northern beans, drained
2 boiling potatoes, cubed and cooked
2 rutabagas, cubed and cooked
2 14½-ounce cans yellow hominy, drained
Salt and freshly ground pepper to taste

In large kettle, simmer pork and corned beef in water for 2 hours or until tender. Add chicken pieces and 1 can of beans; purée the other can of beans in blender or food processor and add to stew. Bring to boil and simmer for 30 minutes. Add potatoes, rutabagas, and hominy; heat thoroughly. Skim fat from top and discard. Correct seasoning; add salt and pepper if necessary.

Serves 8 to 10

Comment: A good after-skiing dish. Portion beef and chicken into each soup bowl and spoon vegetables over.

Chicken Nugget Soup

Nuggets:

2 cups ground uncooked chicken breast
3 tablespoons minced fresh parsley
2 tablespoons grated Parmesan cheese
1 cup fine bread crumbs
¼ teaspoon salt
¼ teaspoon freshly ground pepper
½ teaspoon dried marjoram, crushed
3 egg whites

Combine chicken with parsley, Parmesan cheese, bread crumbs, salt, pepper, marjoram, and egg whites. Refrigerate for 1 hour or until firm enough to shape. Form into 1-inch round nuggets.

Soup:

2 tablespoons vegetable oil
¼ pound fresh mushrooms, sliced
1 cup sliced green onions
1 cup thinly sliced carrots
1 tablespoon fresh lemon juice
½ teaspoon salt
½ teaspoon dried oregano, crushed
¼ teaspoon freshly ground pepper
7 cups chicken broth
1 cup shell macaroni

In large kettle, sauté chicken nuggets in hot oil until golden. Add mushrooms, onions, and carrots; sauté for 3 minutes. Add lemon juice, salt, oregano, and pepper; mix well. Stir in chicken broth and heat to boiling; reduce heat and add macaroni. Cook until chicken nuggets are done and carrots are tender, 15 to 20 minutes. Taste for seasoning. Serve garnished with chopped parsley and sprinkle with Parmesan cheese.

Garnish:

2 tablespoons chopped fresh parsley
¼ cup grated Parmesan cheese

Serves 8

Comment: This nutritious soup is a winner served with a tomato aspic salad and lime sherbet for dessert.

Scotch Broth

2 pounds lamb neck bones
1½ pounds lean boneless lamb, cut into 1-inch cubes
2 quarts chicken broth
½ teaspoon salt
¼ teaspoon freshly ground pepper
1 bay leaf
½ cup pearl barley
3 cloves garlic, minced
2 large potatoes, cut into 1-inch cubes
4 medium carrots, ½-inch thick
4 ribs celery, cut into 1-inch chunks
1 large onion, coarsely chopped
½ cup sliced green onions
1 10-ounce package frozen lima beans
1 teaspoon dried thyme, crushed
¼ cup dry white wine or dry vermouth
2 tablespoons chopped fresh parsley

Garnish:
2 tablespoons chopped fresh parsley

Serves 8 to 10

In large kettle, bring to boil lamb bones, lamb, broth, salt, pepper, and bay leaf. Skim off residue that rises to surface for 15 minutes; reduce heat, cover, and simmer 1½ hours. Remove and discard bones; skim off fat. Stir in barley, garlic, potatoes, carrots, celery, onion, green onions, lima beans, thyme, wine or vermouth, and 2 tablespoons parsley. Return to boil. Reduce heat, simmer covered, 45 minutes or until lamb and vegetables are tender. Discard bay leaf; taste for seasoning. Garnish with 2 tablespoons parsley before serving.

Comment: The lamb flavor is very subtle in this soup. Serve with a Waldorf salad topped with toasted slivered almonds.

Hot Beef Entrées

Burgundy Beef

4 thick slices bacon, cut into 1-inch pieces
4 tablespoons butter or margarine
4 tablespoons vegetable oil
2 cups chopped onions
3 pounds lean beef chuck, cut into 1-inch cubes
½ cup all-purpose flour
1 teaspoon salt
½ teaspoon freshly ground pepper
2 cups sliced carrots
½ cup minced fresh parsley
1 teaspoon dried thyme, crushed
1 bay leaf
1½ cups dry red wine
2 teaspoons instant beef bouillon
4½ cups water
1 tablespoon tomato paste
Freshly ground pepper to taste
1 pound small white onions, fresh or frozen
½ pound fresh mushrooms, stems sliced, caps whole

Fry bacon in 6- to 8-quart Dutch oven over medium-low heat until crisp; remove, drain, and set aside. Add 1 tablespoon each butter or margarine and oil to bacon fat. Stir in chopped onions and brown evenly; remove with slotted spoon and set aside. Dredge beef cubes in a mixture of flour, salt, and ½ teaspoon pepper. Brown beef on all sides in hot fat, ½ pound at a time; add 2 tablespoons each butter or margarine and oil as needed to Dutch oven. As meat is browned remove and set aside. Sauté carrots, ¼ cup parsley, and thyme in fat in Dutch oven, stirring frequently, for 5 minutes. Add browned onions, bay leaf, wine, beef bouillon, 4 cups water, tomato paste, pepper, and meat cubes with juice; bring to boil. Cover and bake in preheated 325°F oven for 1½ hours. Add white onions and remaining ½ cup water; stir gently. Cover and bake for 1 hour longer or until meat is tender and onions cooked. Check once or twice during cooking; stir gently, and add more water if mixture seems too thick. Meanwhile, heat remaining 1 tablespoon butter or margarine and oil. Sauté mushrooms, stirring frequently. Stir mushrooms and reserved bacon into meat mixture; continue baking until heated through. Skim fat from sauce and discard. Spoon into a warmed serving dish and sprinkle with remaining ¼ cup parsley.

Serves 8

Comment: An excellent way to prepare a less expensive cut of meat and have a dish fit for company. Serve with plenty of fluffy white rice or buttered homemade noodles.

Left, clockwise from the top: Jiggs' Corned Beef and Cabbage, see page 23; Stuffed Green Peppers, see page 23; Beef Ragout with Artichokes, see page 14; Indian Tacos, see page 24.

Beef Ragout with Artichokes

5 to 6 tablespoons vegetable oil
2 large onions, quartered and sliced
2 cloves garlic, minced
3 pounds boneless beef chuck roast
⅓ cup all-purpose flour
½ teaspoon salt
½ teaspoon freshly ground pepper
1 teaspoon dried dill weed
1 cup dry red wine
2 cups beef broth (approximately)
20 fresh mushrooms, quartered
¼ cup butter or margarine
1 9-ounce package frozen artichoke
   hearts, thawed and cut into quarters
Biscuits (recipe follows)
¼ cup butter or margarine, melted
¼ cup freshly grated Parmesan cheese

Heat 3 tablespoons vegetable oil in heavy Dutch oven and sauté onions and garlic for 6 minutes; remove with slotted spoon. Remove any gristle and excess fat from meat; cut into bite-size pieces. Dredge meat in flour, salt, and pepper. In skillet, over medium-high heat, brown meat a third at a time, adding remaining oil as needed. Remove meat and set aside as browned. Return all meat to Dutch oven with onions and garlic. Add dill, wine, and enough broth to barely cover. Simmer, covered, approximately 2 hours or until meat is tender. In skillet, sauté mushrooms in ¼ cup butter or margarine for 2 to 3 minutes. Add artichoke hearts; sauté 3 to 4 minutes and add to meat mixture. Place stew in 9×13-inch baking dish. Arrange biscuit dough on top of ragout and bake in preheated 400°F oven for 20 minutes. Remove casserole from oven and brush top of biscuits with ¼ cup melted butter or margarine; sprinkle with grated cheese. Return to oven for 5 minutes.

Biscuits:

3 cups all-purpose flour
1 tablespoon sugar
4½ teaspoons baking powder*
¾ teaspoon salt
¾ teaspoon cream of tartar
¾ cup cold butter or margarine
¾ cup milk
1 egg, lightly beaten

Sift together in bowl, flour, sugar, baking powder, salt, and cream of tartar. With pastry blender cut in butter or margarine until mixture resembles meal; stir in milk and egg. Place dough on lightly-floured surface; knead once or twice and pat into ¾-inch thick square. Cut biscuit dough into squares with floured knife.

*For altitude over 5,000 feet, use 4 teaspoons baking powder. Bake casserole at 425°F.

Serves 6 to 8

Comment: The artichoke hearts and dill give this ragout an unusual flavor. For dessert, try tart lemon sherbet topped with raspberry purée.

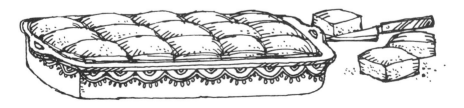

Cheese-Topped Beef Pie

1 pound lean ground beef
1 egg
⅓ cup minced onion
1 cup cracker crumbs
2 tablespoons barbecue sauce
1 teaspoon salt
Dash of freshly ground pepper
1 large onion, thinly sliced
3 tablespoons butter or margarine
⅔ cup sliced celery
⅔ cup chopped green pepper
½ pound fresh mushrooms, sliced
1½ cups shredded sharp Cheddar
  cheese

Heat oven to 400°F. Combine meat, egg, minced onion, ¾ cup cracker crumbs, barbecue sauce, salt, and pepper. Press into bottom and sides of 9-inch pie plate and bake for 15 minutes. Remove from oven; drain fat.* Reduce oven temperature to 350°F. Sauté sliced onion in 1 tablespoon butter or margarine; remove and set aside. Sauté celery and green pepper in 1 tablespoon butter or margarine for 3 minutes; add mushrooms and stir-fry for 3 minutes. Layer sautéed onion on top of hot meat shell; add remaining vegetables.

Top with cheese. Melt remaining 1 tablespoon butter or margarine and combine with remaining ¼ cup cracker crumbs; sprinkle over cheese layer. Return to oven and continue baking for 10 minutes.

*To drain fat from meat shell, lightly hold a saucepan lid over meat and pour off fat.

Serves 6

Comment: A pleasant variation of the familiar cheeseburger. Further enhance with mustards or ketchup, crusty rolls, and a beverage.

Italian Eggplant-Meat Lasagne

2 1-pound eggplants, pared and sliced ¼-inch thick
Salt
1½ pounds lean ground beef
3 tablespoons butter or margarine
3 onions, diced
1 carrot, coarsely grated
½ green pepper, chopped
½ cup diced celery
3 cloves garlic, minced
2 cups tomato sauce
3 tablespoons minced fresh parsley
½ teaspoon dried basil, crushed
½ teaspoon dried oregano, crushed
Salt and freshly ground pepper to taste
3 to 4 tablespoons olive or vegetable oil
1 pound mozzarella cheese, shredded
1 3-ounce Italian pepperoni sausage, thinly sliced

Sprinkle eggplant heavily with salt and set aside for 20 minutes. In large skillet, sauté beef and remove with slotted spoon; set aside. Pour off grease but do not remove bits stuck to skillet. Melt butter or margarine in same skillet; sauté onions, carrot, green pepper, celery, and garlic for 10 minutes or until limp. Add meat, tomato sauce, parsley, basil, oregano, salt, and pepper to taste. Simmer for 15 minutes, covered. Rinse salt from eggplant and press out liquid. Brush slices with olive or vegetable oil and place on greased broiler pan; broil about 4 inches from heat until golden brown. Sprinkle lightly with salt and pepper. Turn and brush with oil; broil other side in same manner. Assemble in greased 9×13-inch casserole. Place a third of the eggplant in first layer, slightly overlapping; follow with a third of the meat sauce, a third of the mozzarella, and half of the pepperoni; repeat layers until all ingredients are used, ending with mozzarella on top. Cover with foil; bake in preheated 350°F oven for 30 minutes or until heated through and cheese has melted.

Serves 8 to 10

Comment: Even non-eggplant lovers will enjoy the flavor. Add garlic bread and an Italian salad for a special meal.

Chinese Steak

1½ pounds boneless sirloin steak
2 cloves garlic, minced
6 tablespoons soy sauce
6 tablespoons dry sherry
2 teaspoons sugar
1 tablespoon minced fresh ginger root
¼ teaspoon freshly ground pepper
2 teaspoons cornstarch
½ pound fresh mushrooms, sliced
1 cup drained bamboo shoots
1 carrot, thinly sliced
1 6-ounce package frozen Chinese pea pods, thawed
6 green onions, cut into 2-inch lengths
2 ribs celery, diagonally sliced
1 green pepper, seeded and sliced
3 tablespoons vegetable oil
Salt and freshly ground pepper to taste

To slice meat, place in freezer until firm but not frozen; cut into slices ⅛-inch thick. Mix garlic, 3 tablespoons soy sauce, 3 tablespoons dry sherry, 1 teaspoon sugar, ginger root, ¼ teaspoon pepper, and cornstarch; pour over meat, mix well, and marinate for 30 minutes. Combine mushrooms, bamboo shoots, carrot, pea pods, green onions, celery, and green pepper in bowl and set aside. Heat 1 tablespoon oil in large skillet or wok. Add a third of the meat and cook, stirring, over high heat for 2 minutes. Remove and keep warm. Continue cooking meat until all is stir-fried, adding 1 tablespoon oil as needed. Heat remaining oil until very hot. Add vegetables and stir-fry over high heat for 5 minutes; add remaining soy sauce and sherry. Sprinkle with remaining 1 teaspoon sugar, salt, and pepper to taste; mix in meat and cook for 2 minutes.

Serves 6

Comment: Serve on heated plates with fluffy white rice and fresh tomato slices.

17

Beerocks

1½ pounds lean ground beef
2 cups shredded cabbage
1 cup sauerkraut, well drained
1 cup minced onion
½ teaspoon paprika
½ teaspoon garlic powder
2 teaspoons instant beef bouillon
1 teaspoon salt
½ teaspoon freshly ground pepper
¾ cup water
2 8-ounce cans refrigerator crescent rolls*
1 egg, lightly beaten
1½ tablespoons water

In large skillet, brown beef and drain off fat. Add cabbage, sauerkraut, onion, paprika, garlic powder, bouillon, salt, pepper, and ¾ cup water; mix well. Cook, uncovered, over medium heat for 20 minutes or until liquid evaporates, stirring occasionally. Separate crescent roll dough into 8 rectangles (do not separate into triangles but firmly press perforations to seal dough). Spoon about ½ cup meat mixture on one end of each rectangle. Mix egg and 1½ tablespoons water together; brush half of the glaze on edges of rectangle. Fold dough over filling; press edges with fork to seal. Place on greased cookie sheet; brush with remaining glaze. Bake in preheated 375°F oven for 12 to 18 minutes or until golden brown. Serve hot or cold.

*If you would prefer to make your own dough, may I suggest the following recipe:

Beerocks Dough:

¾ cup warm water (105° to 115°F)
1 package active dry yeast
2 tablespoons sugar
¾ teaspoon salt
1 cup mashed potatoes
2 eggs
⅓ cup vegetable oil
3 to 3½ cups unbleached flour
1½ tablespoons water

Combine water, yeast, and sugar; let stand 5 minutes or until bubbly. Add salt, potatoes, 1 egg, and oil; beat until well mixed. Add 1½ cups flour and beat for 2 minutes. Stir in remaining flour, ½ cup at a time, until a stiff dough forms. Turn out onto a well-floured surface and knead until smooth and elastic. Let dough rest 15 minutes. Roll out half of the dough into an 18-inch square and cut into quarters. Fill each square with about ½ cup meat mixture. Mix remaining egg and 1½ tablespoons water together; brush glaze on edges of square. Fold dough over filling to form a triangle and press edges with a fork to seal. Repeat to make 8 beerocks. Place on greased cookie sheet. Cover and let rise for 20 to 25 minutes. Brush tops with remaining egg glaze and bake in preheated 375°F oven for 15 to 20 minutes or until golden brown. Serve hot or cold.

Makes 8

Comment: Any leftover dough will make excellent rolls. Make lots of beerocks to freeze for lunchboxes or to take on a hike.

Mexican Beef Dinner

3 tablespoons all-purpose flour
Salt and freshly ground pepper to taste
3 pounds beef chuck, trimmed and
   cut into 1-inch cubes
3 tablespoons vegetable oil
1 teaspoon crushed red pepper or to
   taste
1 large onion, chopped
2 cloves garlic, minced
1 teaspoon ground cumin
1 teaspoon ground coriander
1 28-ounce can solid pack tomatoes,
   chopped and drained (reserve juice)
Beef broth (optional)
1 pound winter squash, sliced 1-inch
   thick and parboiled 15 minutes
3 6-inch zucchini, sliced 1-inch thick
3 ears fresh corn, cut into 2-inch
   pieces
6 small potatoes, scrubbed and
   parboiled 15 minutes

Sprinkle a mixture of flour, salt, and pepper over meat. Heat oil in large Dutch oven or kettle until very hot. Add a third of the meat at a time; as browned remove and set aside. Cook red pepper, onion, and garlic in Dutch oven until limp. Add cumin, coriander, and tomatoes; stir to combine well. Return meat to Dutch oven and add reserved tomato juice to depth of 1 inch. Bring to boil, cover, and bake in preheated 350°F oven for 1 hour and 30 minutes or until meat is tender. During baking add more tomato juice or beef broth to maintain 1-inch depth of liquid. Add yellow squash, zucchini, corn, and potatoes; cover and continue to bake for 30 minutes. Before serving garnish with cilantro or parsley.

Garnish:
2 tablespoons minced fresh cilantro*
   or parsley

*Cilantro is the parsley-like leaves of fresh coriander. It can be purchased in the specialty section of most super markets' produce departments.

Serves 6 to 8

Comment: When serving place the corn on top. Keep the napkins handy! Accompany with heated flour or corn tortillas and plenty of butter.

Polenta Casserole

Polenta:

1 cup yellow cornmeal
4 cups water
1 teaspoon salt

In small bowl, combine cornmeal, 1 cup cold water, and salt. In large heavy saucepan, bring 3 cups water to boil; add cornmeal mixture, stirring constantly. Return to boil and continue to stir until thickened. Cover and continue cooking over low heat for 15 minutes. Pour hot cornmeal into 2 greased 8×8-inch baking dishes. Refrigerate until firm.

Sauce:

1 pound lean ground beef
1 cup minced onion
½ cup minced green pepper
2 cloves garlic, minced
1 16-ounce can tomatoes, undrained
1 8-ounce can tomato sauce
¼ pound fresh mushrooms, sliced
1 teaspoon salt
Few drops hot pepper sauce
1 teaspoon dried oregano, crushed
½ teaspoon dried basil, crushed
6 ounces shredded mozzarella cheese
¼ cup grated Parmesan cheese

Brown meat, onion, green pepper, and garlic in large skillet. Drain off fat. Add tomatoes, tomato sauce, mushrooms, salt, hot pepper sauce, oregano, and basil; mix well. Bring to boil; reduce heat and simmer, uncovered, for 20 minutes, stirring occasionally. Taste for seasoning. To assemble, pour half of the sauce over one dish of polenta and sprinkle with half of the cheeses; unmold second polenta cake and place on top of the first. Cover with remaining sauce and sprinkle with remaining cheeses. Bake in preheated 350°F oven for 30 minutes or until hot and bubbly. Let stand 10 minutes at room temperature before cutting into squares to serve.

Serves 6 to 8

Comment: A serving of this hearty casserole is complemented by assorted fresh vegetables served raw or steamed.

Stir-Fry Asparagus Beef

1 1-pound flank steak cut into ⅛-inch thick strips
Salt and freshly ground pepper to taste
1 tablespoon cornstarch
3 tablespoons dry sherry
¼ cup soy sauce
2 to 3 tablespoons vegetable oil
1 onion, quartered and thinly sliced
2 cloves garlic, minced
1½ pounds asparagus, trimmed and cut into 1½-inch pieces
2 tablespoons water
1 teaspoon sesame oil (optional)
1 teaspoon sugar
3 green onions, minced
1 cup tomato wedges or 1 cup halved cherry tomatoes
1 16-ounce package frozen noodles, cooked
1 tablespoon minced fresh cilantro* or parsley

Place meat strips in bowl and sprinkle with salt and pepper. Mix cornstarch, sherry, and soy sauce together; blend with meat. Marinate 30 minutes or longer. Heat 1 tablespoon vegetable oil in large heavy skillet or wok; add onion and garlic and stir-fry until limp. Remove and set aside. Drain meat; reserve marinade. Add 1 tablespoon oil to skillet and heat until nearly smoking. Add half of the meat and stir-fry until no longer pink. Remove and set aside; repeat with remaining meat. Add more oil to skillet if necessary and stir-fry asparagus for 2 minutes. Add 2 tablespoons water, cover, and steam for 7 to 8 minutes or until just crisp-tender. Add meat, optional sesame oil, sugar, green onions, onion-garlic mixture, and reserved marinade. Stir-fry until sauce thickens and becomes shiny, about 2 to 3 minutes. Add tomato wedges or cherry tomatoes and stir just to coat with sauce; heat slightly. Serve over cooked noodles and sprinkle with cilantro or parsley.

*Cilantro is the parsley-like leaves of fresh coriander. It can be purchased in the specialty section of most super markets' produce departments.

Serves 4 to 6

Comment: Here is a nice combination when asparagus is in season. Pass extra soy sauce if you like. For dessert, serve lemon sherbet and fortune cookies.

Family-Size Pizza Pie

Pastry for 10-inch Double Crust Pie:

2 cups sifted all-purpose flour
¾ teaspoon salt
⅔ cup solid vegetable shortening
5 to 7 tablespoons cold water

Sift flour and salt into bowl. Cut in shortening with pastry blender until size of small peas. Sprinkle water over top and toss with fork until completely moistened. Form into 2 equal-size balls; wrap and chill for 30 minutes.

Filling:

2 eggs
1 pound lean ground beef
1 medium onion, minced
¼ pound fresh mushrooms, sliced
1 15-ounce can tomato sauce
2 tablespoons minced fresh parsley
1 teaspoon dried oregano, crushed
½ teaspoon dried basil, crushed
1 teaspoon salt
¼ teaspoon freshly ground pepper
1 cup grated sharp Cheddar cheese
½ cup grated Parmesan cheese

Roll out half of pastry and place in 9-inch pie pan. Separate one egg and beat white until foamy; brush inside of pastry and set aside. Brown beef and onion and drain off fat; add mushrooms and stir for 5 minutes. Remove from heat and stir in tomato sauce. Beat egg yolk and whole egg together, add to meat mixture with parsley, oregano, basil, salt, and pepper. Pour into pie crust. Sprinkle with Cheddar and Parmesan cheeses. Roll out remaining pastry, cover, and seal. Cut slits for steam to escape. Bake in preheated 400°F oven for 25 minutes. Let set 5 minutes before cutting.

*If you prefer, use frozen pie crusts; thaw 2 9-inch crusts for 15 minutes. Brush bottom crust with beaten egg white. Fill with meat mixture and sprinkle with Cheddar and Parmesan cheeses. Moisten edges of crust with water and carefully tip second pie crust on top; loosen at edges to release from tin. Press edges together with fingers or fork to seal. Cut slits for steam to escape; bake as directed.

Note: When preparing Family-Size Pizza Pie, make 1½ times the Filling recipe and use extra for Stuffed Green Peppers, see page 23.

Serves 4

Comment: For a variation, use mozzarella cheese in place of Cheddar. Turn down the lights and get out the candles!

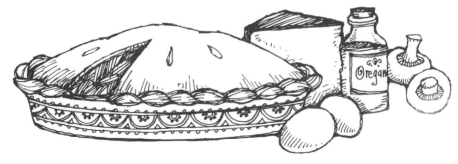

Stuffed Green Peppers

3 green peppers
½ of meat filling plus all of the cheese from Family-Size Pizza Pie recipe (see page 22)

Cut 3 large green peppers in half, remove seeds, and blanch in boiling water for 5 minutes. Drain and fill with meat mixture. Place in greased 8×8-inch baking dish; pour ¼ cup water in bottom of dish. Bake in preheated 350°F oven for 20 minutes. Remove from oven, sprinkle with cheese, and bake 10 minutes longer, or until cheese has melted and filling is heated through.

Serves 6

Comment: Serve with fresh corn on the cob.

Jiggs' Corned Beef and Cabbage

3 pounds corned beef*
1 rib celery
1 teaspoon peppercorns, crushed
4 whole cloves
1 bay leaf
¼ teaspoon crushed red pepper
1 clove garlic, minced
6 boiling potatoes, pared and quartered
6 carrots, halved lengthwise
6 small turnips, halved
6 small onions
1 head cabbage, cut into 6 wedges

Place corned beef in large heavy kettle and cover with water. Bring to boil; lower heat and simmer for 15 minutes. Skim residue from surface as it rises. Add celery, peppercorns, cloves, bay leaf, red pepper, and garlic. Simmer for 3 to 3½ hours or until beef is tender. Add potatoes and carrots; cook for 15 minutes. Add turnips and onions and cook until vegetables are tender; add cabbage during last 10 minutes. Remove celery and bay leaf. Cut meat into thin slices; arrange on large heated platter with vegetables. Spoon some cooking liquid over meat slices just before serving.

*Use corned beef round, if available, as it has less fat than the brisket.

Serves 6 to 8

Comment: Serve with a variety of mustards and whole grain breads for an attractive presentation.

Indian Tacos

1 pound lean ground beef
½ cup chopped onion
1 15-ounce can red kidney beans or chili beans, drained (reserve liquid)
1 8-ounce can tomato sauce
⅓ cup chicken broth
2 teaspoons chili powder or to taste
½ teaspoon ground cumin or to taste
1 teaspoon salt
¼ teaspoon freshly ground pepper
Indian or Cornmeal Fry Bread (recipes follow)
4 to 5 cups coarsely shredded iceberg lettuce
½ cup sliced green onions, including some tops
2 tomatoes, peeled, seeded, and chopped
1½ cups shredded sharp Cheddar cheese

In skillet, sauté meat until lightly browned; add onion and sauté until tender. Stir in beans, tomato sauce, chicken broth, chili powder, cumin, salt, and pepper. Add reserved bean liquid if too thick; simmer 15 minutes. Remove and discard any grease that has accumulated. To serve, spoon meat mixture over rounds of Fry Bread and top with lettuce, onions, tomatoes, and cheese.

Serves 6 to 8

Indian Fry Bread:

4 to 5 cups unsifted all-purpose flour
2 tablespoons baking powder (this is correct!)
2 tablespoons vegetable oil
1½ teaspoons salt
2 tablespoons sugar
1¾ cups warm water
Vegetable oil

Thoroughly mix together 4 cups flour, baking powder, 2 tablespoons oil, salt, sugar, and water. Mixture will be a batter; let stand at room temperature for 30 minutes. Use remaining flour to knead dough until smooth and elastic; let rest 15 minutes. Roll ¼-inch thick and cut into 4-inch rounds. Make a slit in the center of each round with a knife to help bread fry faster and to keep from becoming soggy. Pour 1 inch vegetable oil in skillet; heat over moderate heat to 375°F. Dough dropped in will immediately begin to puff up and turn golden brown. Turn rounds of dough once and fry until puffy and golden brown. Drain on paper towels.

Cornmeal Fry Bread:

2 cups unsifted all-purpose flour
2 cups yellow cornmeal

Thoroughly mix flour and cornmeal. Use in place of 4 cups flour in Indian Fry Bread recipe, then proceed with that recipe.

Makes 16 to 20 4-inch rounds

Comment: These are a favorite at American Indian festivals. Prepare either or both fry breads ... make extra to serve with honey.

CUMIN

Red
Kidney
Beans

m Howe

Pork and Lamb Entrées

Eggs and Ham in Mornay Sauce

5 hard-cooked eggs
2 tablespoons real butter
2 tablespoons all-purpose flour
1 cup milk
Salt and cayenne pepper to taste

Cut the eggs in half, remove yolks, and rub them through a sieve. Set aside seived yolks and egg white halves. Melt butter in saucepan and add flour; cook and stir for 3 minutes. Add milk, salt, and pepper. Cook and stir until thick.

Add 3 tablespoons sauce to egg yolks; reserve remaining sauce.

1 tablespoon real butter
¾ cup minced fresh mushrooms
1 tablespoon minced shallots
2 teaspoons minced fresh parsley
2 teaspoons minced fresh chives or green onion
½ teaspoon Dijon mustard
⅛ teaspoon dried tarragon, crushed
Salt and freshly ground pepper to taste
1 teaspoon real butter, softened

Melt 1 tablespoon butter in saucepan over medium-high heat. Add mushrooms and shallots; stir, cooking until dry. Add remaining ingredients. Stir and add to yolk mixture; blend well. Stuff halved egg whites with mixture.

5 asparagus spears, cooked crisp-tender
5 slices boiled ham, thinly sliced
1 cup grated natural Swiss cheese
½ cup half-and-half
½ cup soft bread crumbs
1 tablespoon real butter

Place an asparagus spear on each slice of ham, and sprinkle with 1 tablespoon cheese; roll. Add remaining cheese and half-and-half to reserved sauce; heat and stir until cheese is melted. Spread ⅓ cup sauce in 8×8-inch baking dish. Arrange stuffed eggs and rolled ham over this layer. Cover with

remaining sauce. Sauté bread crumbs in butter; sprinkle over sauce. Bake in preheated 350°F oven for 20 minutes, just enough to heat through without overcooking eggs.

Serves 5

Comment: Nice for a brunch or ladies luncheon. I suggest serving with popovers and plenty of butter.

Left, from the top: Greek Supper Pie, see page 33; Eggs and Ham in Mornay Sauce, see page 27; Choucroute Garni (Sauerkraut Garnished with Meat), see page 32.

Irish Lamb Stew

2 tablespoons vegetable oil or bacon
   drippings
2½ pounds boneless lean shoulder of
   lamb, cut into cubes
⅓ cup all-purpose flour
2 teaspoons salt
¼ teaspoon freshly ground pepper
8 small onions
2 ribs celery, sliced
3 carrots, sliced
3 turnips, cut into thin wedges
½ teaspoon dried marjoram, crushed
½ teaspoon dried thyme, crushed
2 cups water
1 10-ounce package frozen peas,
   thawed
2 tablespoons cider vinegar
2 tablespoons sugar
½ teaspoon dried mustard
2 cups seasoned mashed potatoes*
2 tablespoons butter or margarine,
   melted

Heat vegetable oil or bacon drippings in large Dutch oven. Dredge lamb in flour seasoned with salt and pepper; brown over medium-high heat until no longer pink. Add onions, celery, carrots, turnips, marjoram, thyme, and water; stir to combine. Bring to boil, cover, and simmer for 1½ hours or until meat is tender. Skim fat from surface. Add peas to lamb mixture and cook 5 minutes. Blend vinegar, sugar, and mustard; stir into lamb. Spoon into deep 3-quart baking dish. Top with potatoes and brush with melted butter or margarine. Bake in preheated 450°F oven for 10 minutes or until potatoes are lightly browned.

*Mashed potatoes are so much better if prepared just before placing on top of the stew mixture.

Serves 8

Comment: Complement with sliced avocado and grapefruit segments arranged on crisp greens and topped with vinaigrette dressing. Parsleyed biscuits are great with the extra gravy.

Chorizo Enchiladas

1 pound chorizo sausage, crumbled
6 eggs, lightly beaten
1 cup grated Monterey Jack cheese
2 10-ounce cans mild or hot
  enchilada sauce
12 corn tortillas
2 cups grated sharp Cheddar cheese

Garnish:
Shredded iceberg lettuce

Brown sausage; drain well and return to skillet. Add eggs; cook, stirring constantly, until just set. Remove from heat; stir in Monterey Jack cheese. Spoon enough enchilada sauce into 9×13-inch baking dish just to film the bottom. Warm the tortillas one at a time in skillet over medium heat until pliable, turning once; fill each tortilla with approximately 3 tablespoons filling. Roll and place seam side down in baking dish; cover with remaining sauce and Cheddar cheese. Cover dish with foil and bake in preheated 350°F oven for 20 minutes or until cheese melts and sauce bubbles. To serve, garnish with shredded lettuce.

Makes 12

Comment: Try this recipe from our Mexican neighbors. Good for a brunch—the eggs give it a breakfasty flavor. Serve with fresh fruit.

Spinach and Sausage Frittata

½ pound bulk Italian sausage
2 tablespoons olive oil
½ pound fresh mushrooms, sliced
½ cup minced onion
1 10-ounce package frozen spinach,
  thawed and well drained
6 eggs, lightly beaten
1 cup grated Romano cheese
1 cup grated provolone cheese
2 cloves garlic, minced
1 teaspoon dried basil, crushed
½ teaspoon dried marjoram, crushed
Freshly ground pepper to taste

Brown sausage in large skillet; remove and drain. Discard grease from skillet; add olive oil and heat until a light haze forms. Add mushrooms and onions; stir-fry over high heat until lightly browned. Stir in spinach and cook 3 minutes. Remove from heat. In bowl combine eggs, ⅔ cup Romano cheese, ⅓ cup provolone cheese, garlic, basil, marjoram, and pepper to taste. Stir in sausage and vegetables. Pour into well-greased 10-inch pie pan and sprinkle with mixture of remaining ⅓ cup Romano and ⅔ cup provolone cheese. Bake in preheated 350°F oven until set, about 25 minutes. Be careful not to overbake or the frittata will become dry.

Serves 6 to 8

Comment: A tasty blend of meat, vegetables, and eggs. Serve with sliced tomatoes and toasted English muffins.

French Bean Pot Cassoulet

3 cups dried white beans, soaked
overnight and drained
2 teaspoons salt
1 teaspoon dried thyme, crushed
1 bay leaf
4 dashes hot pepper sauce
½ pound Polish or garlic sausage

Bring beans to boil in fresh water to cover; simmer for 2 minutes. Set aside for 1 hour. Drain and cover with fresh water; bring to boil. Add salt, thyme, bay leaf, hot pepper sauce, and whole Polish or garlic sausage, which has been pricked with fork 3 or 4 times. Bring to boil, reduce heat, cover, and simmer for 30 minutes. Remove sausage; set aside. Continue to simmer beans for 1 hour, covered, or until beans are tender but not mushy. Add more water if necessary to keep beans barely immersed while cooking.

½ pound lean salt pork, sliced
2 pounds lean shoulder of lamb, cut
into 1-inch cubes
2 large onions, chopped
3 cloves garlic, minced
Salt and freshly ground pepper to taste
2 cups chicken broth
¼ cup tomato paste
2 whole chicken breasts, boned
1 tablespoon butter or margarine

In small saucepan, blanch salt pork in boiling water for 5 minutes; drain. In large skillet, lightly brown salt pork; remove and set aside. Add lamb to skillet and lightly brown; remove and set aside. Pour off all but 2 tablespoons fat from skillet; add onions and garlic and sauté, stirring, until light brown. Sprinkle lightly with salt and pepper. Add chicken broth, tomato paste, and bring to boil; return pork and lamb to skillet and simmer gently, covered, for 1 hour. Cut chicken breasts into diagonal slices about 1-inch thick; sauté in 1 tablespoon butter or margarine until meat loses pink color; sprinkle lightly with salt and pepper and set aside.

To assemble:

3 tablespoons minced fresh parsley
1½ cups soft bread crumbs
⅓ cup real butter, melted

Drain beans and reserve juice; set aside. Skin and slice sausage 1-inch thick and set aside. Grease 6-quart Dutch oven and layer a third of the beans, half of the sausage, half of the lamb mixture, a third of the beans, remainder of the sausage and lamb, all of the chicken, and top with remainder of the beans. Add reserved bean juice to just cover contents of Dutch oven; bring to simmer on top of stove. Mix parsley, bread crumbs, and ⅓ cup melted butter; sprinkle over top of beans. Bake, uncovered, in preheated 400°F oven for 30 to 40 minutes or until lightly browned on top. Serve immediately.

Serves 8 to 10

Comment: This takes a bit of time to prepare but once assembled it only takes a short time to bake. Serve with garlic French bread and a tossed garden green salad.

Bacon and Swiss Quiche

Pastry for 10-inch Single Crust Pie
(see page 57)
8 slices bacon, cut into 1-inch pieces, fried crisp, and drained
2 cups half-and-half
1½ cups grated natural Swiss cheese
½ teaspoon salt
¼ teaspoon ground nutmeg
¼ teaspoon paprika
Hot pepper sauce to taste
4 eggs, lightly beaten
3 to 4 green onions, sliced, including some tops

Prepare pie crust; prick bottom and sides with fork and bake in preheated 425°F oven for 8 minutes or until almost done, but not brown. Sprinkle bacon evenly over bottom of pie shell. In heavy saucepan heat half-and-half; add cheese and stir until melted. Season with salt, nutmeg, paprika, and hot pepper sauce to taste. Pour ½ cup mixture into beaten eggs, stirring constantly. Slowly stir this mixture back into hot mixture, and add green onions. Pour into pie shell. Bake at 325°F for 35 to 45 minutes. Quiche is done when knife inserted 3 inches from edge comes out clean.

Serves 6

Comment: If you wish you can prepare, bake, and refrigerate the quiche ahead of time. Reheat at 325°F for 15 to 20 minutes until heated through. Serve with sliced tomatoes and herb dressing on a bed of salad greens. A honey-laced fruit cup finishes the meal.

Choucroute Garni
(Sauerkraut Garnished with Meat)

2 tablespoons lard or vegetable oil
2 onions, minced
3 cloves garlic, minced
4 16-ounce cans sauerkraut, drained
1 pound lean salt pork
1 pig knuckle or foot, sliced in half
10 juniper berries
8 whole allspice
8 peppercorns
Salt to taste
1 bay leaf, cut in half
3 cups water
1 cup dry white wine
1 pound Polish sausage
6 smoked pork chops
6 new potatoes, unpared, scrubbed, and parboiled 15 minutes
6 thick frankfurters or thick garlic sausages

Heat lard or vegetable oil in heavy skillet; add onions and garlic and sauté until limp. Rinse sauerkraut in fresh water until acidity is removed if you prefer a less pronounced flavor. Drain well and blend sauerkraut with onion mixture. In large Dutch oven, layer a third of the sauerkraut. Slice salt pork ½-inch thick and layer half of it on sauerkraut; add half of pig knuckle or foot. Mix together juniper berries, allspice, and peppercorns. Sprinkle half of this mixture over the pork layer. Sprinkle with salt to taste and lay ½ bay leaf in center. Repeat layers, ending with sauerkraut. Add water and wine; bring to boil on top of stove and cover tightly. Place in preheated 400°F oven and bake for 45 minutes to 1 hour. Slice sausage into 8 pieces and place over sauerkraut; top with pork chops, potatoes, and franks or garlic sausage. Return to oven, cover, and bake for an additional 30 minutes or until meats and potatoes are tender. To serve, heap the sauerkraut in the middle of large heated platter and garnish with the meats and potatoes.

Serves 6 to 8

Comment: Traditionally served with an assortment of mustards, pumpernickle bread, and a pitcher of beer.

Greek Supper Pie

Tomato Topping:

1 tablespoon butter or margarine
¼ cup chopped green pepper
1 tablespoon all-purpose flour
1 8-ounce can tomato sauce

Melt butter or margarine in saucepan; add green pepper and sauté for 3 minutes. Blend in flour; cook and stir for 3 minutes. Add tomato sauce and stir until thickened. Boil 1 minute, remove from heat, and set aside.

Meat Filling:

3 tablespoons butter or margarine
½ cup minced onion
1½ pounds ground lamb
1 15-ounce can tomato sauce
1 teaspoon salt
½ teaspoon freshly ground pepper
¾ teaspoon ground cinnamon

Melt butter or margarine in large skillet; sauté onion. Add lamb and cook until just pink. Drain off fat; add tomato sauce, salt, pepper, and cinnamon. Simmer 10 minutes, stirring occasionally. Remove from heat.

Macaroni Layer:

1¾ cups uncooked elbow macaroni
3 eggs
2 cups grated sharp Cheddar cheese
Salt and freshly ground pepper to taste

Cook macaroni according to package instructions until barely tender; drain. While macaroni is cooking, beat eggs until light and lemon-colored in large bowl. Add 1½ cups cheese to drained macaroni, tossing until cheese melts. Fold macaroni-cheese mixture into beaten eggs. Lightly sprinkle with salt and pepper; spoon half of this into greased 9×9-inch baking dish. Spoon meat mixture over macaroni; layer with remaining macaroni and thickened Tomato Topping. Bake in preheated 350°F oven for 30 minutes or until heated through. Top with remaining ½ cup cheese and continue baking until cheese melts, about 3 to 5 minutes. Let set 10 minutes before cutting.

Serves 6 to 8

Comment: This looks a little complicated but it isn't; I've broken up the recipe to make it flow smoothly. The flavor is outstanding — even the children like it. Serve with a lime and cucumber salad similar to the one in my MENU PLANNER COOKBOOK.

Italian Sausage Pizza

Crust:
1 package active dry yeast
1¼ cups lukewarm water
4 cups all-purpose flour
1 teaspoon salt
⅛ teaspoon cayenne pepper
   (optional)
2 tablespoons olive or vegetable oil

Allow 1¼ hours for mixing and baking time. Dissolve yeast in lukewarm water. Add flour, salt, optional cayenne, and oil; mix thoroughly. Knead on lightly-floured surface until smooth, about 5 minutes. Cover with a cloth and let rest for 20 minutes. Oil or grease 2 12- or 14-inch pizza pans or 4 8- or 9-inch pie pans. Divide dough in half or in quarters, depending on size of pans used. Roll each piece of dough to fit pan; crimp edges and brush lightly with olive or vegetable oil.

Toppings and Sauce:
1 pound bulk Italian sausage
   (medium-hot)
1 16-ounce can tomatoes, drained
   (reserve ¾ cup juice)
1 6-ounce can tomato paste
2 cloves garlic, minced
1 tablespoon dried oregano, crushed
1 tablespoon dried basil, crushed
1½ cups shredded mozzarella cheese
½ cup grated Romano cheese

Fry sausage over low heat about 10 minutes or until meat is lightly browned; drain and set aside. Combine reserved tomato juice, tomato paste, garlic, oregano, and basil; mix well. Spread sauce evenly over prepared crusts. Cut tomatoes in small pieces and place over sauce. Add sausage and mozzarella cheese; sprinkle Romano cheese over each. Bake in preheated 425°F oven for 15 minutes or until crusts are golden brown.

Makes 2 large or 4 medium pizzas

Comment: Making your own crust is easy. The toppings can be varied to suit your tastes. Serve with an Italian green salad and a carafe of red wine.

34

Layered Soufflé Pie

3 eggs, separated
1 cup dairy sour cream
½ cup all-purpose flour
1½ cups shredded sharp
   Cheddar cheese
1 cup shredded Monterey Jack cheese
1 10½-ounce can cream of chicken
   soup
1 teaspoon minced onion
3 tablespoons all-purpose flour
Dash of freshly ground pepper
½ pound bacon, cut into 1-inch
   pieces, fried, and drained
1 10-ounce package frozen peas
   or green beans, cooked according
   to package instructions

Beat egg whites until stiff; set aside. Blend egg yolks, sour cream, ½ cup flour, and 1 cup Cheddar cheese together; fold into egg whites. Pour half of batter into greased 10-inch pie pan. Sprinkle with ½ cup Monterey Jack cheese. Bake in preheated 375°F oven for 10 minutes. Remove from oven; reduce heat to 350°F. Combine soup, onion, 3 tablespoons flour, pepper, bacon, prepared peas or green beans, and remaining ½ cup Monterey Jack cheese. Spoon into center of baked soufflé shell. Pour remaining batter over filling. Sprinkle with ½ cup Cheddar cheese. Bake for 25 to 30 minutes or until golden brown. Let stand 5 minutes before serving.

Serves 6 to 8

Comment: This is a soufflé you don't have to worry about falling. Cut into wedges to serve and accompany with half an avocado filled with vinaigrette dressing.

Ham and Cheese Crepes

Crepes:

1 cup all-purpose flour
⅛ teaspoon salt
3 eggs
2 tablespoons real butter, melted
1½ cups milk
Additional butter for frying

Sift flour and salt into small bowl. Beat in eggs, one at a time, until batter is smooth; stir in butter and milk. Let stand 2 hours or refrigerate overnight. Before making crepes, let batter stand at room temperature at least 1 hour. Butter hot 6-inch skillet and pour in a generous tablespoon of batter or enough to thinly coat bottom of pan. Quickly rotate pan to coat bottom evenly with batter. Cook crepe briefly until underside is golden brown; flip over, and stack crepes on warm platter until all batter is used.

Filling:

5 tablespoons real butter
5 tablespoons all-purpose flour
½ teaspoon salt
1½ cups milk
2 egg yolks, lightly beaten
1½ cups finely diced ham
1 cup shredded natural Swiss cheese
1 teaspoon Dijon mustard
Cayenne pepper to taste
2 tablespoons real butter, melted
¼ cup grated Parmesan cheese

Heat 5 tablespoons butter in saucepan and add flour; cook, stirring, for 3 minutes. Add salt and milk; cook, stirring, until thickened. Add some of the hot sauce to yolks and mix thoroughly; return to hot sauce while stirring. Remove from heat and stir in 1 cup ham, Swiss cheese, mustard, and cayenne to taste. Spread 12 crepes thickly with filling and roll loosely. Arrange seam side down in buttered oven-proof serving dish.

Sprinkle top of crepes with reserved ½ cup ham; pour melted butter over crepes and dust with Parmesan cheese. Bake in preheated 400°F oven for 25 minutes or until crepes are hot and bubbly.

Serves 6

Comment: These just melt in your mouth! A lovely luncheon dish served with buttered asparagus and lemon sherbet.

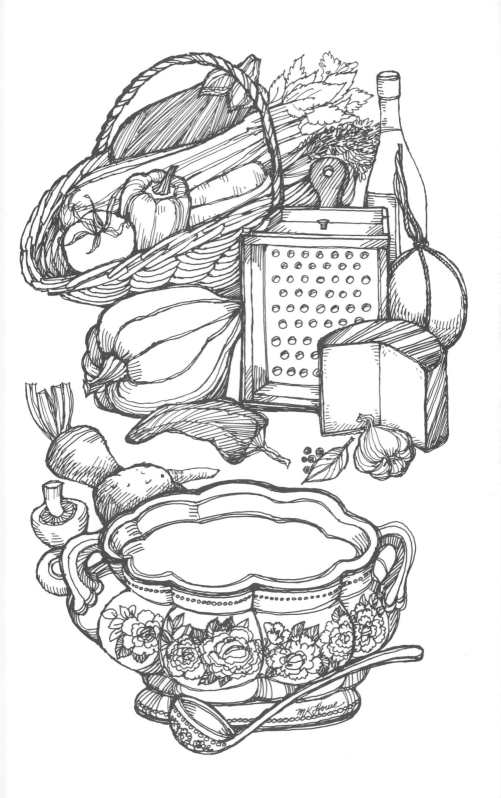

Hot Chicken and Seafood Entrées

Hot Chicken Salad Pie

Cheddar Cheese Pie Shell:

1 cup all-purpose flour
½ teaspoon salt
⅓ cup plus 1 tablespoon solid vegetable shortening
½ cup grated sharp Cheddar cheese
2 tablespoons cold water

Combine flour and salt. Cut in shortening until consistency of coarse meal. Stir in cheese and sprinkle with water. Toss mixture together, adding more water if necessary to moisten flour. Form dough into ball; wrap in plastic or foil and chill for 1 hour. Roll on lightly-floured board and place in 10-inch pie plate; crimp edges securely and prick bottom and sides of shell with fork. Chill for additional 30 minutes. Bake in preheated 475°F oven for 8 minutes. Let cool.

Chicken Salad Filling:

3 cups cubed cooked chicken breast
1½ cups coarsely sliced celery
1 cup finely diced green pepper
¼ cup minced onion
¼ cup diced pimiento
½ cup real mayonnaise
½ cup dairy sour cream
1 tablespoon fresh lemon juice
½ teaspoon salt
Freshly ground pepper to taste
1 egg white, lightly beaten
1 cup crushed potato chips
½ cup grated sharp Cheddar cheese

Combine chicken, celery, green pepper, onion, and pimiento. Thoroughly mix mayonnaise, sour cream, lemon juice, salt, and pepper; blend into chicken mixture. Brush Cheddar Cheese Pie Shell with egg white; fill with chicken salad. Mix potato chips and cheese; sprinkle over top of pie. Bake in preheated 450°F oven for 20 minutes. If crust browns too fast, cover with foil for final minutes of baking.

Serves 6

Comment: The delicate cheese crust goes well with this filling. Leftover turkey could be used in place of chicken. I like serving a molded cranberry salad as an accompaniment.

Left from the top: Salmon and Asparagus Shortcake, see page 47; Potted Chicken, see page 49; New Orleans Shrimp Creole, see page 54.

Chicken Casserole with Light Cream Sauce

3 cups cooked cubed chicken
1 cup sliced celery
¼ pound fresh mushrooms, quartered
2 cups chicken broth
½ cup sliced green onions
2 cups cooked rice
¼ cup diced pimiento
2 cups soft bread crumbs
2 tablespoons minced fresh parsley
4 eggs, lightly beaten
½ to 1 teaspoon salt
Freshly ground pepper to taste
¼ teaspoon paprika
¼ cup butter or margarine
½ cup slivered almonds
2 cups unflavored bread croutons

In large bowl mix all but last 3 ingredients. Place in well-greased 9×13-inch baking dish. In large skillet, melt butter or margarine, add almonds and sauté until lightly browned; add croutons and stir until well-coated. Sprinkle over top of casserole and bake in preheated 350°F oven for 30 to 40 minutes. Serve with the following sauce.

Light Cream Sauce:

¼ cup real butter
¼ pound fresh mushrooms, sliced
¼ cup all-purpose flour
2 cups chicken broth
2 egg yolks
¼ cup half-and-half
¼ teaspoon salt
1 tablespoon fresh lemon juice
Few drops hot pepper sauce
1 tablespoon minced fresh parsley

Melt butter in saucepan and add mushrooms; sauté for 5 minutes, stirring. Add flour and stir for 3 minutes. Stir in chicken broth and bring to boil; simmer for 10 to 15 minutes, stirring occasionally, until thickened. In bowl, beat the egg yolks and add half-and-half, salt, lemon juice, and hot pepper sauce; add some of the hot mushroom sauce, stirring well. Pour egg mixture into mushroom sauce, and stir for 3 to 5 minutes over low heat. Blend in parsley before serving.

Serves 8 to 10

Comment: Make this casserole ahead and enjoy your own party! May be doubled for a larger group. A platter of crisp-tender broccoli flowerets accented with cherry tomatoes will enhance the casserole. For dessert, sprinkle fresh orange slices with orange liqueur and top with toasted coconut just before serving.

Party Turkey Casserole

1 pound thin spaghetti, cooked until barely tender
1 cup grated Parmesan cheese
6 tablespoons dry sherry
Salt and freshly ground pepper to taste
1 tablespoon butter or margarine
1 cup cooked ham, cut into 1-inch long julienne strips
¾ pound fresh mushrooms, thinly sliced
6 cups cooked turkey, cut into 1-inch long julienne strips
Rich Cream Sauce (recipe follows)
¼ cup minced fresh parsley
¼ cup minced fresh chives

Drain cooked spaghetti and toss with ½ cup Parmesan cheese and 2 tablespoons sherry. Spread spaghetti mixture into greased 9×13-inch baking dish; sprinkle lightly with salt and pepper to taste. Heat butter or margarine in large skillet; sauté ham and mushrooms for 5 minutes, turning frequently. In large bowl, mix sautéed ham and mushrooms with turkey strips; toss. Stir into hot Rich Cream Sauce and heat well; stir in remaining 4 tablespoons sherry, parsley, and chives. Taste and correct seasoning, if necessary. Spoon mixture carefully over spaghetti. Sprinkle top with

remaining ½ cup Parmesan cheese. Bake in preheated 325°F oven for 25 to 30 minutes; brown top quickly under broiler.

Rich Cream Sauce:

6 tablespoons butter or margarine
6 tablespoons all-purpose flour
5 cups half-and-half
1 teaspoon salt
½ teaspoon freshly ground white pepper
1 teaspoon paprika
4 egg yolks, lightly beaten

Melt butter or margarine in medium saucepan; add flour and cook, stirring, for 3 minutes. Add half-and-half; stir over medium heat until sauce has thickened, about 10 minutes. Add salt, pepper, and paprika. Stir ½ cup sauce into egg yolks; quickly stir egg yolk mixture into hot sauce. Cook, stirring, for 3 minutes.

Serves 12 to 14

Comment: A real crowd pleaser. Make half a recipe with leftover turkey for a smaller group. Accompany with a tray of raw vegetables.

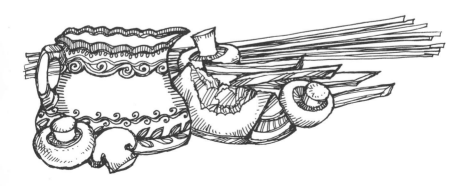

Shrimp or Crab Crepes

½ pound shrimp or crab, cleaned and cooked
3 tablespoons butter or margarine
4 green onions, thinly sliced
2 ribs celery, thinly sliced
½ cup sliced fresh mushrooms
3 tablespoons all-purpose flour
½ teaspoon salt
Several drops hot pepper sauce
1 cup half-and-half
4 Italian tomatoes, peeled and thinly sliced
1 egg yolk
8 prepared crepes (Ham and Cheese Crepes, see page 36)
1 tablespoon real butter, cut into 8 slivers
⅓ cup grated Parmesan cheese

Serves 4

Prepare shrimp or crab; set aside. In medium saucepan, heat 3 tablespoons butter or margarine and add onions, celery, and mushrooms; sauté, stirring until limp. Add flour and stir for 3 minutes. Stir in salt, hot pepper sauce, and half-and-half; simmer, stirring, until thickened. Add tomatoes and continue to cook for 5 minutes. Beat egg yolk and add some of the hot mixture; return to saucepan and cook for 3 minutes, stirring. Stir in shrimp or crab. Fill each of the 8 crepes with about 3 tablespoons filling. Place seam side down in well-greased 7×11-inch baking dish. Top each with a sliver of butter and sprinkle with Parmesan cheese. Bake in preheated 375°F oven for 10 minutes or until hot and bubbly.

Chicken Acapulco

4 pounds frying chicken pieces
1 tablespoon vegetable oil
1 onion, minced
2 cloves garlic, minced
6 peppercorns
½ pound chorizo sausage
2 cups chicken broth
1 10-ounce can tomatoes and green chilies
3 carrots, diced
3 7-inch zucchini, diced
¼ cup raisins
3 whole jalapeno peppers

Garnish:
1 whole orange, halved and thinly sliced

Serves 6 to 8

In Dutch oven, sauté chicken pieces in vegetable oil until browned; remove and set aside. Pour off all but 2 tablespoons grease from pan. Add onion, garlic, and peppercorns. Remove sausage from casing, add to onion mixture and sauté for 5 to 7 minutes; drain off grease. Add chicken broth and tomatoes; simmer, uncovered until sauce is reduced by a third. Return chicken to the mixture. Cover and simmer for 20 minutes. Add carrots and cook for 5 minutes. Add zucchini, raisins, and peppers; cook for an additional 10 minutes or until chicken is tender and vegetables are crisp-tender. Garnish with orange slices to bring out the sweetness of the raisins.

Comment: This dish has an exciting sweet-hot flavor which can be changed by adjusting the amount of jalapeno peppers used.

Chicken-Cilantro Enchiladas

2 whole chicken breasts, about 2
  pounds
2 cups water
1 onion, sliced
1 clove garlic, minced
2 to 3 sprigs of fresh cilantro* or
  parsley
1⅓ cups chicken broth
2 10-ounce cans mild enchilada sauce
4 cups coarsely grated Monterey Jack
  cheese
8 green onions, thinly sliced
2 tablespoons chopped fresh cilantro*
  leaves
Salt and freshly ground pepper to taste
Few drops hot pepper sauce
12 corn tortillas

**Garnish with any or all
of the following:**
Shredded iceberg lettuce
Dairy sour cream
Guacamole or sliced avocado

Bring chicken breasts to boil in water with onion, garlic, and cilantro or parsley sprigs; reduce heat and simmer until tender, about 10 minutes. Remove chicken from broth when cool and shred meat; strain broth. Add 1⅓ cups broth to enchilada sauce; set aside. For filling, combine chicken, 2 cups cheese, green onions, and cilantro leaves with salt, pepper, and hot pepper sauce to taste. Add 1 cup enchilada sauce to moisten. Warm tortillas on hot griddle or skillet until flexible, turning once; dip in enchilada sauce and lay flat. Fill with 2 to 3 tablespoons chicken filling; roll and place in 9×13-inch greased baking dish, seam side down. Spoon remaining enchilada sauce over tortillas and sprinkle evenly with remaining 2 cups cheese. Cover baking dish with foil; place in preheated 350°F oven for about 20 minutes or until sauce bubbles and cheese melts. Garnish with your choice of lettuce, sour cream, and guacamole or sliced avocado.

*Cilantro is the parsley-like leaves of fresh coriander. It can be purchased in the specialty section of most super markets' produce departments.

Serves 6

Comment: Enchiladas may be made ahead, refrigerated, and brought to room temperature before baking.

Jambalaya

2 ounces cubed salt pork, blanched*
¾ pound ham, diced
2 medium onions, chopped
1 green pepper, chopped
1 clove garlic, minced
2 16-ounce cans tomatoes, drained
  (reserve juice)
2 tablespoons tomato paste
1 teaspoon sugar
1 tablespoon chopped fresh parsley
1 teaspoon salt
Freshly ground pepper to taste
1 bay leaf (optional)
4 cups liquid (reserved tomato juice
  plus chicken broth)
4 cups cooked chicken, cut into 1-inch
  pieces
1½ cups raw rice, rinsed
1 tablespoon real butter
½ pound raw medium shrimp, peeled

In Dutch oven, sauté pork cubes for 5 to 7 minutes; remove salt pork, drain, and reserve fat. Add ham and lightly brown in 1 tablespoon reserved fat; set aside. Add additional 1 tablespoon fat; sauté onions, green pepper, and garlic. Add tomatoes, tomato paste, sugar, parsley, salt, pepper, and optional bay leaf; add liquid and bring to boil. Put chicken, ham, and salt pork back in Dutch oven; add rice, stir, and cover. Simmer until rice is tender and dry. In small skillet, melt butter; sauté shrimp for 3 or 4 minutes or until they become opaque. Carefully stir shrimp into rice and heat through. Remove optional bay leaf before serving.

*To blanch, cover with cold water in small saucepan. Bring to boil and simmer 3 to 5 minutes; drain.

Serves 6

Comment: A Gulf Coast favorite . . . adapted for a buffet menu. A crisp, fresh green salad and a crusty loaf of bread are good accompaniments.

Clam and Shrimp Risotto

2 tablespoons dry vermouth
1 7-ounce can minced clams, drained (reserve liquid)
1 4½-ounce can tiny Alaskan shrimp, drained (reserve liquid)
¼ cup real butter
½ cup minced green onions
1 cup short-grain Italian Arborio rice or medium grain rice
3 cups hot chicken broth
1 cup tiny green peas
2 tablespoons minced fresh parsley
Salt and freshly ground pepper to taste

Garnish:
2 tablespoons chopped fresh parsley
½ cup grated Parmesan cheese

Pour vermouth over clams and shrimp in small bowl; set aside. Melt butter in medium saucepan and stir in green onions; simmer for 3 minutes. Add rice and stir for 5 minutes. Add 1 cup hot chicken broth; simmer, covered, stirring every few minutes until broth is nearly absorbed, about 10 minutes. Stir in additional ½ cup chicken broth; continue cooking, stirring until nearly absorbed and rice becomes creamy. Stir in reserved liquid from clams and shrimp. Cook, stirring; add ¼ cup broth each time liquid has been absorbed. Add only as much liquid as rice will absorb. Meanwhile, cook peas in 2 tablespoons chicken broth for 3 minutes. Stir clams, shrimp, and peas into rice; heat through. Add 2 tablespoons minced parsley, salt, and pepper to taste. Garnish with 2 tablespoons chopped parsley sprinkled on top just before serving. Pass the Parmesan cheese separately.

Serves 6

Comment: Serve as soon as prepared to enjoy the creamy texture for which risotto is famous. Serve with a relish tray of fresh raw vegetables.

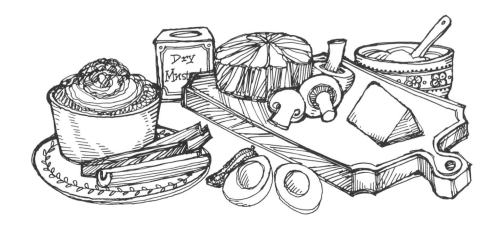

Tuna Nests

¼ pound fresh mushrooms, sliced
4 tablespoons butter or margarine
1 7-ounce can tuna, drained and flaked
2 tablespoons all-purpose flour
1 cup milk
¾ cup grated American cheese
¼ teaspoon salt
Freshly ground pepper to taste
Deviled Eggs (recipe follows)
½ cup crushed corn flakes

Sauté mushrooms in 1 tablespoon butter or margarine until limp. Add to tuna and toss lightly. Divide and spoon into 4 lightly buttered custard cups; flatten surface. Melt 2 tablespoons butter or margarine in skillet; add flour and cook for 3 minutes, stirring constantly. Add milk and cook until thick, stirring. Add ½ cup cheese, salt, and pepper; stir until cheese melts and blends into sauce. Pour over tuna mixture. Top with Deviled Eggs; sprinkle with remaining cheese. Melt remaining 1 tablespoon butter or margarine and toss with corn flakes; sprinkle around eggs. Bake in preheated 350°F oven 20 minutes or until heated through. Do not overcook.

Deviled Eggs:

4 hard-cooked eggs
1 tablespoon real mayonnaise
1 tablespoon butter or margarine, melted
1 tablespoon chopped sweet pickle or pickle relish
½ teaspoon cider vinegar
¼ teaspoon dry mustard or to taste
⅛ teaspoon salt or to taste
Freshly ground pepper to taste

Halve eggs lengthwise. Remove and mash yolks; combine with mayonnaise, butter or margarine, pickle or pickle relish, vinegar, mustard, salt, and pepper. Fill whites.

Serves 4

Comment: Your children will love this one! It is a fun dish for a change of pace. Serve with carrot and celery sticks.

Salmon and Asparagus Shortcake

1 15½-ounce can red salmon, drain, skin, bone, and flake (reserve liquid)
3 tablespoons minced onion
4 tablespoons butter or margarine
3 tablespoons all-purpose flour
1½ cups liquid (reserved salmon liquid plus milk)
½ teaspoon salt
Few drops hot pepper sauce
1 tablespoon fresh lemon juice
1 cup shredded sharp Cheddar cheese
Shortcake (recipe follows)
⅓ cup minced bread and butter pickles
¾ pound fresh asparagus spears, cooked

Garnish:
Lemon slices
Fresh parsley sprigs

Shortcake:
2 cups all-purpose flour
1 tablespoon baking powder
½ teaspoon cream of tartar
½ teaspoon salt
6 tablespoons cold butter or margarine, thinly sliced
½ cup milk
1 egg, lightly beaten
½ cup shredded sharp Cheddar cheese

Place flaked salmon in small saucepan; set aside. In medium saucepan, sauté onion in 3 tablespoons butter or margarine until limp. Stir in flour and continue to cook for 3 minutes. Add liquid, salt, hot pepper sauce, and lemon juice; stir over medium-high heat until thickened, about 5 minutes. Stir in cheese until melted. Add half of the prepared sauce to salmon in small saucepan; blend and heat through. Spoon salmon mixture on one shortcake, top with second shortcake, and pour remaining cheese sauce over top. Sprinkle with pickles and surround with hot asparagus. Melt remaining 1 tablespoon butter or margarine and drizzle over asparagus. Garnish with lemon slices and parsley sprigs. To serve cut into wedges and place 3 or 4 asparagus spears beside each serving.

Sift flour, baking powder, cream of tartar, and salt into bowl.* With fork or pastry blender, cut in butter or margarine until mixture resembles meal. Stir in milk, egg, and cheese. Place dough on lightly-floured surface. Knead once or twice and pat into 2 8-inch rounds. Bake on well-greased baking sheet in preheated 400°F oven for 15 minutes or until golden brown.

Note: For altitudes 5,000 feet or over, use only 2½ teaspoons baking powder and bake at 425°F.

*Can be made in food processor. Place dry ingredients in bowl with steel blade in place. Turn on/off twice. Add butter or margarine. Turn on/off two or three times. Add milk, egg, and cheese through funnel. As soon as dough mounds on blade, remove from machine and place on floured surface. Knead once or twice and pat into 2 8-inch rounds.

Serves 6

Comment: I've had many compliments on this appetizing luncheon or supper dish. I suggest accenting with fresh tomatoes cut into wedges.

Chicken-Shrimp Paella

2 pounds frying chicken pieces
4 tablespoons olive oil
½ pound Italian or chorizo sausage, cut into ½-inch slices
¼ teaspoon dried crushed red pepper
½ pound raw shrimp, peeled
1 10-ounce can whole clams, drained (reserve juice)
1 large onion, minced
½ green pepper, coarsely chopped
2 small cloves garlic, minced
1 16-ounce can Italian plum tomatoes, drained, seeded, and chopped (reserve juice)
Salt and freshly ground pepper to taste
1½ cups chicken broth
1 6-ounce package saffron rice
1 small zucchini, thinly sliced
1 10-ounce package frozen peas, thawed

Garnish:
½ red pepper, sliced or 1 pimiento, sliced

Serves 6

Brown chicken pieces in 2 tablespoons olive oil in large oven-proof skillet or paella pan. Remove chicken with slotted spoon. Brown sausage lightly; remove and set aside. Sauté red pepper for 1 minute. Add shrimp and clams to skillet and heat 1 minute while turning. Remove and set aside. Add 2 tablespoons oil to skillet; sauté onion, green pepper, and garlic for 5 to 7 minutes. Stir in tomatoes, reserved juice, salt, and ground pepper to taste; simmer 10 to 15 minutes to thicken. Add chicken and sausage to pan, simmer covered 10 minutes. Stir in broth, clam juice, rice, and zucchini; heat to boiling. Place pan on middle shelf of preheated 375°F oven and bake for 30 minutes, partially covered. Increase oven temperature to 400°F. Stir peas into rice; add shrimp and clams, pushing partially into rice. Garnish top with slices of red pepper or pimiento and continue to bake for 15 minutes, uncovered, or until liquid is absorbed and rice is tender.

Comment: A version of the famous Spanish dish. Additional shrimp or clams in the shell may be added for garnish. A custard flan is traditional for dessert.

Potted Chicken

1 3- to 4-pound whole frying chicken
½ cup real butter, melted
2 teaspoons salt
½ cup dry vermouth
½ cup chicken broth
Few drops hot pepper sauce
6 new potatoes, well scrubbed (cut in half, if large)
6 carrots, cut into 2-inch pieces
12 small onions or 1 16-ounce package frozen small onions
½ pound large fresh mushrooms
½ cup chopped celery
1 tablespoon cornstarch
1 tablespoon cold water

Set oven at broil. Place rack in lowest position. Remove all fat from chicken cavity; truss and place on back on oven broiling pan. Broil about 20 to 30 minutes, basting chicken frequently with melted butter; turn until browned all over. Remove chicken to large Dutch oven. Sprinkle with salt; add vermouth, chicken broth, and hot pepper sauce along with drippings from broiler pan. Cover and simmer over low heat for 45 minutes. Add potatoes, carrots, onions, and mushrooms in layers around chicken; sprinkle top with celery. Cover and bake in preheated 350°F oven for 1 hour or until chicken and vegetables are tender. Remove chicken to cutting board, carve, and place on warm platter. Surround with vegetables; cover. Blend cornstarch with cold water, and add to cooking liquid; bring to boil. Simmer, stirring constantly until thickened, about 3 to 5 minutes. Serve as accompaniment to chicken.

Serves 6

Comment: This one reminds me of good, wholesome, "growing-up" flavors. For a dessert, I like a nice wedge of strawberry pie. Try the recipe I have in my FAMILY FAVORITES COOKBOOK.

Salmon in Shells

14 conchiglie rigati grandi (super shell pasta), about 6 ounces
2 large carrots, thinly sliced
2 cups minced onion
¼ cup water
2 10-ounce packages frozen tiny green peas
Salt and freshly ground pepper to taste
½ cup minced green pepper
¾ cup minced celery
2 tablespoons minced fresh parsley
½ teaspoon dried basil, crushed
2 tablespoons butter or margarine
1 15½-ounce can red salmon, drain, skin, bone, and flake (reserve liquid)
Béchamel Sauce (recipe follows)
1 cup milk
1 cup shredded mozzarella cheese

Cook pasta according to package directions; drain and set aside. Simmer carrots, 1 cup onions, and ¼ cup water in saucepan for 10 to 15 minutes until carrots are almost crisp-tender. Add peas and simmer for 2 minutes or until liquid has evaporated. Salt and pepper lightly. In skillet, sauté remaining 1 cup onion, green pepper, celery, parsley, and basil in butter or margarine for 3 minutes. Carefully blend in salmon and ¾ cup Béchamel Sauce. Taste for seasoning. Fill each shell, mounding slightly. Grease 9×13-inch baking dish; pour ½ cup milk in bottom. Add half of the carrots and peas, and arrange filled shells on top of this mixture; surround with remaining vegetables. Thin remaining Béchamel Sauce with ½ cup milk, spoon over shells and vegetables, top with mozzarella. Cover with foil; place in preheated 350°F oven for 20 to 30 minutes or until heated through. Remove foil and place under broiler for 3 minutes or until lightly browned.

Béchamel Sauce:

6 tablespoons butter or margarine
6 tablespoons all-purpose flour
2 teaspoons instant chicken bouillon
3 cups liquid (reserved salmon liquid plus milk)
2 egg yolks, beaten
Salt and freshly ground pepper to taste

Heat butter or margarine in saucepan and add flour; stir for 3 minutes. Add chicken bouillon and liquid; cook, stirring occasionally, until sauce thickens, about 10 to 15 minutes. Stir some of the hot sauce into beaten yolks, return mixture to saucepan, stir over heat for 3 minutes. Season with salt and pepper to taste. Remove from heat.

Serves 6 to 8

Comment: Truly a complete meal. I suggest cantaloupe á la mode for a refreshing dessert.

Poulard Basquaise

10 small white onions
1 tablespoon butter or margarine
¼ pound salt pork, cubed
Salt and freshly ground pepper to taste
4 pounds frying chicken pieces
¾ pound fresh mushrooms, quartered
1 eggplant, pared and cut into
   ½- × 3-inch julienne strips
4 large tomatoes, peeled, seeded, and
   quartered
2 green peppers, quartered and sliced
3 cloves garlic, minced
1 teaspoon dried basil, crushed
½ teaspoon dried thyme, crushed
½ teaspoon dried marjoram, crushed
1 bay leaf
½ cup dry vermouth
½ cup chicken broth
2 tablespoons cornstarch
2 tablespoons cold water

In small skillet, sauté onions in butter or margarine, turning until glazed and lightly browned. Set aside. Sauté salt pork cubes in large skillet until browned; remove, drain, and set aside. Reserve fat. Salt and pepper chicken pieces; sauté in pork fat until browned. Place in 9×13-inch baking dish. Discard all but 3 tablespoons of fat and sauté mushrooms, eggplant, tomatoes, green pepper, and garlic for 3 minutes. Sprinkle with basil, thyme, and marjoram; add bay leaf and reserved salt pork, mixing well. Lightly sprinkle with salt and pepper. Place mixture around chicken pieces in baking dish; add sautéed onions. To the skillet in which chicken and vegetables were cooked, add vermouth and chicken broth; bring to boil, scraping up any crusty bits and pour over chicken and vegetables. Cover and cook in preheated 350°F oven for 50 to 60 minutes.

To serve, arrange chicken and vegetables on a warmed platter. Pour juices into a saucepan. Combine cornstarch and cold water; whisk mixture into juices. Bring to boil, whisking constantly, until clear and thickened. Serve with chicken and vegetables.

Serves 8 to 10

Comment: Fluffy white rice and crusty rolls add the finishing touch.

Chinese Chicken and Almonds

1 cup sliced onion
½ pound fresh mushrooms, sliced
2 tablespoons butter or margarine
½ pound fresh bean sprouts
1 8-ounce can sliced water chestnuts, drained
1 cup sliced celery
2 teaspoons minced fresh ginger root or to taste
3 cups diced cooked chicken
2 cups chicken broth
3 tablespoons cornstarch
¼ teaspoon salt or to taste
¼ cup soy sauce
4 cups hot cooked rice
2 tablespoons minced fresh parsley or cilantro*
¼ cup diced pimiento
⅔ cup toasted slivered almonds

Sauté onions and mushrooms in butter or margarine in 12-inch skillet until partially cooked, about 3 minutes. Stir in bean sprouts, water chestnuts, celery, ginger root, chicken, and ¼ cup broth. Bring to boil and remove from heat. In small saucepan, stir cornstarch and salt into soy sauce and remaining chicken broth; bring to boil, stirring, until thickened. Put thin layer of sauce in bottom of greased 9×13-inch baking dish and spread rice over sauce. Stir parsley or cilantro and chicken mixture into remaining sauce and blend well; spoon over rice. Bake, covered, in preheated 350°F oven for 15 minutes. Sprinkle top with pimiento and almonds and bake another 5 minutes or until hot and lightly browned on top.

*Cilantro is the parsley-like leaves of fresh coriander. It can be purchased in the specialty section of most supermarkets' produce departments.

Serves 8

Comment: Nice and crunchy. I suggest passing the soy sauce for a more Oriental flavor.

Salmon-Cheese Pie

Pastry for 10-inch Double Crust Pie (see page 22)
1 egg white, lightly beaten
1 15½-ounce can red salmon, drain, skin, bone, and flake (reserve liquid)
⅓ cup sliced celery
⅓ cup sliced green onions
⅓ cup sliced green pepper
3 tablespoons butter or margarine
3 tablespoons all-purpose flour
1½ cups liquid (salmon liquid plus milk)
1 teaspoon dried dill weed
½ teaspoon salt
Few drops hot pepper sauce to taste
3 eggs, lightly beaten
2 tablespoons dry sherry
⅔ cup grated sharp Cheddar cheese

Roll out half of the pastry; fit into pan and brush with beaten egg white. Reserve remaining egg white. Wrap and refrigerate remaining pastry for top crust. Place salmon in bowl and toss with celery, green onions, and green pepper. Heat butter or margarine in saucepan and stir in flour; cook for 3 minutes, stirring. Slowly add liquid and stir until thickened. Remove from heat; stir in dill, salt, hot pepper sauce, eggs, sherry, ⅓ cup cheese, and salmon mixture. Brush pastry crust again with reserved egg white; sprinkle with remaining ⅓ cup cheese and top with salmon mixture. Roll remaining pastry dough into a 12-inch round; place over filling and adjust to fit. Seal and flute edges; cut slits for steam to escape. Bake in preheated 425°F oven for 30 minutes or until crust is golden brown. Let cool 10 minutes before cutting.

Serves 6

Comment: Great eating, both hot and cold! It would be a fine meal at home or on a picnic accompanied by fresh raw vegetables or fruit.

New Orleans Shrimp Creole

½ cup butter or margarine
1 pound raw shrimp, peeled
¼ cup dry vermouth
2 cups coarsely chopped onion
2 cups coarsely chopped green
  pepper
1½ cups coarsely chopped celery
4 cloves garlic, minced
Salt and freshly ground pepper to taste
½ teaspoon dried rosemary, crushed
½ teaspoon dried thyme, crushed
½ teaspoon dried sage, crushed
1 bay leaf
¼ cup minced fresh parsley
½ teaspoon crushed red pepper
2 16-ounce cans tomatoes, cut into
  quarters (reserve juice)
2 teaspoons sugar
7 to 8 cups hot cooked rice

Heat 1 tablespoon butter or margarine in large skillet. Add shrimp and sauté 2 minutes, stirring; add vermouth and cook 1 minute longer. Remove shrimp and drippings to bowl. Heat remaining butter or margarine in skillet and sauté onion, chopped green pepper, celery, and garlic for 10 minutes, stirring. Add salt, pepper, rosemary, thyme, sage, bay leaf, minced parsley, red pepper, tomatoes with juice, and sugar. Simmer, uncovered, for 20 minutes. Add all but 4 shrimp; cook just to heat through. To serve, place rice in serving bowl, pour shrimp sauce over; top with reserved shrimp. Garnish with green pepper slices and parsley.

Garnish:
Green pepper slices
Sprigs of fresh parsley

Serves 10 to 12

Comment: One pound of shrimp and 10 guests! Somewhere between a soup and a stew. Crusty French bread is a perfect accompaniment.

Vegetables and Salads

Creamy Shrimp Salad Pie

Pastry for 10-inch Single Crust Pie:

1½ cups all-purpose flour
½ teaspoon salt
½ cup solid vegetable shortening
4 to 5 tablespoons cold water

Sift flour and salt into bowl. Cut in shortening with pastry blender until size of small peas. Sprinkle water over top and toss with fork until completely moistened. Form dough into ball and roll out on lightly-floured surface from center to edge until ⅛-inch thick. Fit into pan and flute edge; prick the crust with fork. Refrigerate 1 hour or place in freezer for 30 minutes. Bake in preheated 450°F oven for 10 to 12 minutes or until golden brown; cool before adding filling.

Filling:

1 3-ounce package lemon-flavored gelatin
1 cup boiling water
1 3-ounce package cream cheese, softened
¼ cup real mayonnaise
½ cup cold water
2 tablespoons cider vinegar
½ cup whipping cream
½ cup chopped celery
1½ cups cooked medium shrimp, cut in half lengthwise (reserve 8)
½ cup minced green pepper
3 tablespoons chopped pimiento
2 tablespoons minced green onion
2 tablespoons chopped fresh parsley

Dissolve gelatin in boiling water. Gradually add to cream cheese, blending well. Add mayonnaise, cold water, and vinegar; blend well and chill until partially set. Whip cream to soft peaks. Whip gelatin mixture until slightly fluffy, about 2 or 3 minutes; fold in whipped cream. Fold in celery, shrimp, green pepper, pimiento, onion, and 1 tablespoon parsley. Chill gelatin mixture until it mounds when spooned. Pour into prepared shell. Chill until firm. Garnish with remaining 8 shrimp and chopped parsley. Cut in wedges to serve.

Serves 6 to 8

Comment: For a luncheon or Sunday supper, serve with buttered broccoli or asparagus spears.

Left, clockwise from the top: Mexican Meat and Vegetable Salad, see page 60; Crisp Spinach Salad, see page 64; Tuna and Fruit Salad, see page 64; Carrot Salad, see page 61.

Broccoli Salad

1½ pounds fresh broccoli (stems pared), cooked and cut into bite-size pieces
5 hard-cooked eggs, coarsely chopped
1 cup salad olives
1 red onion, coarsely diced
1 cup coarsely diced celery
Salt to taste
1 cup real mayonnaise
1 teaspoon fresh lemon juice
½ teaspoon dry mustard
Freshly ground pepper to taste

Combine broccoli, eggs, olives, onion, and celery; salt lightly and toss. Chill. To serve, spoon into serving dish. Blend mayonnaise, lemon juice, mustard, salt, and pepper; spoon over broccoli mixture. Garnish with pimiento strips.

Garnish:
Pimiento strips

Serves 6

Comment: Serve with tuna or chicken sandwiches for a heartier meal.

Chicken Chow Mein Salad

1½ cups cubed cooked chicken
1 cup cooked peas
6 hard-cooked eggs, sliced
1 cup diced celery
½ cup coarsely chopped green pepper
¼ cup chopped pimiento
¾ cup real mayonnaise
2 tablespoons minced onion
1 teaspoon fresh lemon juice or to taste
½ teaspoon salt or to taste
¼ teaspoon freshly ground pepper
1 5-ounce can chow mein noodles

Combine chicken, peas, eggs, celery, green pepper, and pimiento; toss gently just to mix. Combine mayonnaise, onion, lemon juice, salt, and pepper; blend into chicken mixture. Refrigerate. To serve, mound chicken salad in center of serving platter and surround with chow mein noodles. Garnish with additional strips of green pepper and pimiento.

Garnish:
Green pepper strips
Pimiento strips

Serves 4 to 6

Comment: For dessert serve tangy pineapple sherbet.

Italian Whole Meal Salad

1 7-ounce can albacore tuna, drained
2 teaspoons fresh lemon juice
1 big bunch romaine lettuce, crisped
½ pound capacallo* or boiled ham, thinly sliced
¾ pound thinly sliced provolone
¾ pound cotto salami, thinly sliced
½ pound fresh mushrooms, thinly sliced
1 8-ounce jar marinated artichoke hearts or 3 fresh artichokes, cooked, quartered, with choke and leaves removed
½ pound cherry tomatoes
Cauliflowerets, cut into slices
Celery, cut into julienne strips
Carrot, cut into julienne strips
Cucumber, cut into julienne strips
Pitted green and ripe olives

Sprinkle tuna with lemon juice. Arrange bite-size pieces of romaine lettuce on individual salad plates; decoratively place any or all of the meats and vegetables on lettuce leaves in equal portions. Pass Italian Dressing separately when served.

Italian Dressing:
1 cup olive oil
2 small cloves garlic, minced
⅓ cup red wine vinegar
2 tablespoons minced fresh parsley or cilantro** or 1 tablespoon of each
1 teaspoon salt
Freshly ground pepper to taste

Whip dressing ingredients in blender or food processor.

*Capacallo can be found in your delicatessen.

**Cilantro is the parsley-like leaves of fresh coriander. It can be purchased in the specialty section of most supermarkets' produce departments.

Serves 6

Note: Try your own combination of cheeses, meats, or vegetables.

Comment: Crusty Italian bread served in a basket lined with a checkered red napkin would add a festive touch.

Mexican Meat and Vegetable Salad

Marinated Vegetables:

4 tomatoes, peeled, seeded, and coarsely chopped
1 cucumber, pared, seeded, and coarsely chopped
8 green onions, minced
1½ cups vegetable oil
⅓ cup white vinegar
1 clove garlic, minced
1 8-ounce can mild taco sauce
2 tablespoons chopped green chilies
¼ cup sugar
½ teaspoon dried oregano, crushed
½ teaspoon celery seed
¼ teaspoon salt
¼ teaspoon freshly ground pepper
5 tomatoes, peeled and cut into wedges

Place chopped tomatoes, cucumber, and green onions in glass container. In blender or food processor, blend vegetable oil, vinegar, garlic, taco sauce, chilies, sugar, oregano, celery seed, salt, and pepper. Pour marinade over chopped vegetables and refrigerate, covered, for several hours or overnight. Two hours before serving, carefully stir tomato wedges into marinade mixture.

Crisp iceberg lettuce leaves
⅓ pound ham, cut into julienne strips
⅓ pound cooked white meat turkey or chicken, cut into julienne strips
⅓ pound Jarlsburg cheese, cut into julienne strips
3 hard-cooked eggs, cut into quarters
½ cup pitted ripe olives

To serve, arrange lettuce leaves in serving dish. Using slotted spoon, place marinated vegetables on lettuce leaves. Surround with meats, cheese, eggs, and olives. Pass remaining marinade separately.

Serves 6 to 8

Comment: This is my favorite meat and vegetable salad, with the flavors of our neighbors to the south. Can be accented nicely with a basket of tortilla chips.

Carrot Salad

1 pound carrots, coarsely grated
1 cup raisins
1 cup sweetened coconut flakes
1 cup crushed pineapple, drained
1 cup real mayonnaise
2 tablespoons undiluted frozen orange
   juice
1 cup chopped cashews or salted
   Spanish peanuts
Crisp iceberg lettuce leaves

In large bowl mix carrots, raisins, coconut, and crushed pineapple. Gently fold in mayonnaise which has been blended with orange juice. Chill, covered, for 2 hours. Blend in ⅔ cup cashews or peanuts. Place salad on lettuce leaves and sprinkle with remaining cashews or peanuts.

Serves 6 to 8

Comment: The saltiness of the nuts gives a nice contrast to the sweetness of the salad.

Broccoli-Cauliflower Soufflé

2 tablespoons butter or margarine
½ cup minced onion
⅓ cup minced celery
2 tablespoons minced fresh parsley
1 pound fresh broccoli, stems pared
1 small cauliflower
2 tablespoons water
2 cups cooked rice
1 10½-ounce can chicken-mushroom
   soup
3 tablespoons dry vermouth
1 teaspoon dried Italian herb
   seasoning, crushed
Salt and freshly ground pepper to taste
6 eggs, separated
2 cups grated sharp Cheddar cheese
½ teaspoon salt
¼ teaspoon cream of tartar

Melt butter or margarine in large saucepan. Add onion, celery, and parsley; stir for 2 to 3 minutes. Cut broccoli and cauliflower into bite-size flowerets; thinly slice broccoli stems. Add broccoli, cauliflower, and water to saucepan; cover and simmer for 8 minutes. Stir in rice, soup, vermouth, and Italian herb seasoning; add salt and pepper to taste. Place mixture in greased 2-quart baking dish. Bake in preheated 400°F oven for 20 minutes. Meanwhile, beat egg yolks until thick and lemon-colored; stir in cheese. In another bowl, beat whites until frothy; add ½ teaspoon salt and cream of tartar. Beat until stiff but not dry. Stir in yolk mixture. Spoon over top of vegetables; return mixture to oven for 15 to 20 minutes or until puffed and nicely browned on top.

Serves 6 to 8

Comment: I suggest the addition of an orange salad with thin slices of Spanish onion topped with Italian dressing for an economical and easy luncheon.

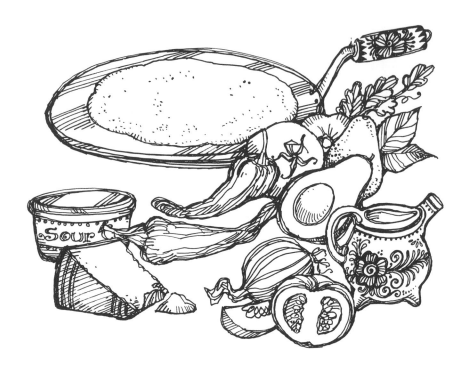

Green Chili-Vegetable Enchiladas

1 8-ounce can diced green chilies, well drained
2 cups dairy sour cream
1 cup grated Monterey Jack cheese
6 tablespoons chopped onion or green onions
6 tablespoons milk
12 corn tortillas
1½ cups grated longhorn Cheddar cheese
Crisp iceberg lettuce, shredded
Taco sauce

Garnish:
Avocado slices
Chopped tomatoes

In bowl, mix chilies into sour cream; add Monterey Jack cheese, onions, and 2 tablespoons milk, blending well. Warm tortillas on griddle until soft and flexible, turning once. Fill each with 2 or 3 tablespoons sour cream mixture. Roll each tortilla and place seam side down in greased 9×13-inch baking dish. When all enchiladas are made, thin leftover sauce with remaining 4 tablespoons milk. Pour this mixture over enchiladas. (Mixture will be a little thin.) Top with grated cheese, shredded lettuce, and taco sauce. Cover baking dish with foil and bake for 20 to 30 minutes in preheated 350°F oven or until cheese melts and sauce bubbles. Remove from oven and garnish with avocado slices and chopped tomatoes.

Serves 6

Comment: THEY ARE DELICIOUS! The method of softening the tortillas is easier and lower in calories than using hot oil.

Gypsy Salad

1 green pepper, quartered and thinly
   sliced
½ medium onion, thinly sliced
1 cup cooked green peas
½ pound fresh mushrooms, thinly
   sliced
1 cup thinly sliced celery
Chiffonade Dressing (recipe follows)
1 6-ounce slice cooked ham
1 6-ounce slice cooked beef
1 6-ounce slice natural Swiss cheese
1 6-ounce slice sharp Cheddar cheese
Crisp iceberg lettuce leaves

Mix pepper, onion, peas, mushrooms, and celery with Chiffonade Dressing; refrigerate, covered, for 1 to 2 hours before serving. Meanwhile cut ham, beef, and cheeses into julienne strips. At serving time, using slotted spoon, arrange marinated vegetables on individual plates lined with lettuce leaves; surround with meats and cheeses. Pour remaining marinade dressing into pitcher and pass separately.

Chiffonade Dressing:

1½ cups olive or vegetable oil or half
   of each
½ cup cider vinegar or fresh lemon
   juice
1 teaspoon Dijon mustard
1 teaspoon dried basil, crushed
1 teaspoon dried thyme, crushed
1 teaspoon dried marjoram, crushed
1 teaspoon salt
¼ teaspoon freshly ground pepper
4 hard-cooked eggs, chopped
⅓ cup minced fresh parsley
2 tablespoons chopped fresh chives
2 tablespoons minced green onion

Blend all ingredients together and use as directed.

Serves 4 to 6

Comment: Use different varieties of meats and cheeses for a change. I especially enjoy sour dough rolls with this combination.

Tuna and Fruit Salad

2 7-ounce cans albacore tuna, drained
3 Red Delicious apples, cored and
  diced (unpared)
1½ teaspoons fresh lemon juice
1½ cups sliced celery
3 tablespoons sliced green onion
4 sweet red cherry peppers, thinly
  sliced
⅔ cup real mayonnaise
½ cup plain yogurt
1 tablespoon capers, drained
Several drops hot pepper sauce
1 tablespoon real butter
½ cup sunflower seed
Crisp iceberg lettuce leaves
1 fresh pineapple, sliced

Break tuna into large chunks. Sprinkle apples with lemon juice. In large bowl, toss together tuna, apples, celery, onion, and cherry peppers. Cover and refrigerate. Blend mayonnaise, yogurt, capers, and hot pepper sauce together in small bowl; cover and refrigerate 2 hours or more. In small skillet, melt butter; sauté sunflower seed until golden. Remove and set aside. Just before serving, toss tuna mixture with dressing. Line salad bowl with lettuce, mound salad in center, and garnish with slices of pineapple. Sprinkle sunflower seed over the top.

Serves 6 to 8

Comment: This salad can be served in a pineapple shell accompanied with assorted crackers.

Crisp Spinach Salad

8 slices bacon, cut into 1-inch pieces
½ pound fresh spinach, stemmed
  and torn into bite-size pieces
4 hard-cooked eggs, chopped
3 green onions, sliced, including some
  tops
½ cup shredded natural Swiss cheese
½ cup garlic croutons (optional)
½ cup real mayonnaise
3 tablespoons plain yogurt
3 tablespoons fresh lemon juice
1½ teaspoons Dijon mustard
¼ teaspoon ground nutmeg
Salt and freshly ground pepper to taste

Fry bacon until crisp; drain and reserve fat. Keep prepared spinach at room temperature. In large bowl combine bacon, spinach, eggs, onion, Swiss cheese, and optional croutons. Blend mayonnaise, yogurt, lemon juice, mustard, nutmeg, salt, and pepper. Drizzle spinach mixture with 3 tablespoons reserved bacon fat; add mayonnaise mixture and toss to coat.

Serves 6

Comment: Serve with buttery hot muffins and brownie sundaes for dessert.

Oriental Vegetable Omelette

2 tablespoons vegetable oil
1 carrot, cut into thin julienne strips, 2 inches long
6 green onions, thinly sliced, including some tops
1 rib celery, thinly sliced
1 clove garlic, minced
1 tablespoon minced fresh ginger root
½ cup water
2 to 4 tablespoons soy sauce
1 teaspoon cornstarch
1 tomato, peeled and cut into thin wedges

Heat vegetable oil until very hot in heavy skillet. Stir-fry carrot, green onions, celery, garlic, and ginger root for 5 minutes. Mix water and soy sauce into cornstarch; add to vegetable mixture, stirring until thickened. Remove from heat; add tomato wedges, cover, and keep hot.

Omelette:

4 eggs
3 tablespoons water
Salt and freshly ground pepper to taste
2 tablespoons butter or margarine

Break eggs into bowl; beat in water, salt, and pepper. Heat butter in heavy skillet about 8 inches in diameter; pour in eggs. As outer edges set, carefully push to center, tilting pan so uncooked egg can flow to bottom. When top is firmed to your liking, slide the omelette onto heated platter. Spoon hot vegetables and sauce over the top.

Serves 2 to 3

Comment: Garnish this colorful, tasty omelette with sliced green onions. Serve with sausage patties and a thick slice of toast.

Turkey-Mandarin Orange Salad

1 teaspoon fresh lemon juice
1 Red Delicious apple, unpared,
   cored, and diced
4 cups cubed cooked turkey
1 cup sliced celery
⅓ cup finely sliced green onions
½ teaspoon salt
Freshly ground pepper to taste
¾ cup real mayonnaise
6 tablespoons whipping cream,
   whipped
2 tablespoons grated coconut
1 teaspoon grated orange rind
2 teaspoons curry powder (optional)
1 16-ounce can Mandarin orange
   segments, chilled and drained
½ cup salted cashews
Crisp iceberg lettuce leaves

Sprinkle lemon juice on diced apple. In large bowl toss together apple, turkey, celery, onions, salt, and pepper until well mixed. In small bowl blend mayonnaise, whipped cream, coconut, orange rind, and optional curry powder. Blend into turkey mixture and chill. Just before serving blend in Mandarin oranges and ¼ cup cashews. Place salad on lettuce leaves to serve. Chop the remaining cashews and use as a garnish.

Serves 6 to 8

Comment: Use fresh sliced nectarines in season instead of canned Mandarin oranges. Serve with a variety of flavored melba toasts.

Sandwiches and Fillings

Open-Faced Chicken-Asparagus Sandwich

Softened real butter
6 slices Italian bread, toasted
Real mayonnaise
6 large slices cooked chicken breast
Salt and freshly ground pepper to taste
6 hard-cooked eggs, sliced
18 cooked asparagus spears, drained
2 cups White Sauce (recipe follows)
12 slices bacon, cooked crisp and
   drained
3 tablespoons minced fresh parsley

Lightly butter toasted bread; spread with mayonnaise and place on greased jelly roll pan. Place chicken slices on each and sprinkle lightly with salt and pepper. Layer with egg slices and top each with 3 asparagus spears. Spoon White Sauce over each slice of toast and place in preheated 400°F oven for 10 minutes. Place 2 slices of bacon on each and return to oven for 3 minutes to heat. Remove from oven and sprinkle each sandwich with parsley just before serving.

White Sauce:
3 tablespoons real butter
3 tablespoons all-purpose flour
1 teaspoon instant chicken bouillon
2 cups milk
¼ to ½ teaspoon salt
Few drops hot pepper sauce

Melt butter in saucepan; blend in flour and continue stirring for 3 minutes. Add instant chicken bouillon and milk. Over medium-high heat, continue to stir and cook until thickened. Taste for seasoning and add salt and hot pepper sauce.

Serves 6

Comment: Serve for a luncheon or light supper. Start off with consommé and finish with a scoop of pecan ice cream dusted with grated chocolate.

Left, clockwise from the top: Dagwood Pork Sandwich, see page 71; Open-Faced Ham Salad Sandwich, see page 70; Mexican Steak Sandwich, see page 73; Salmon Salad Sandwich, see page 70.

Open-Faced Ham Salad Sandwich

2 cups finely diced ham
2 cups finely shredded cabbage
1 cup coarsely shredded carrots
½ cup diced celery
3 tablespoons minced onion
2 hard-cooked eggs, chopped
½ cup real mayonnaise
½ cup dairy sour cream
1½ tablespoons cream style
  horseradish or to taste
1 teaspoon Dijon mustard
8 frankfurter rolls, split in half
8 tomato slices

In medium bowl, combine ham, cabbage, carrots, celery, onion, and eggs. Combine mayonnaise, sour cream, horseradish, and mustard; blend into ham mixture. Spread filling on opened rolls and top each with a tomato slice; garnish with pickle slices and olives.

Garnish:
Bread and butter pickle slices
Pitted ripe olives

Serves 8

Comment: Assemble sandwich, wrap in foil, and take on a picnic or hike.

Salmon Salad Sandwich

1 15½-ounce can red salmon,
   drain, bone, and flake
¾ cup minced celery
1 small cucumber, chopped
3 hard-cooked eggs, chopped
1 tablespoon minced onion
¾ cup real mayonnaise
1 tablespoon fresh lemon juice
2 teaspoons Dijon mustard
¼ teaspoon dried dill weed or to taste
⅛ teaspoon freshly ground nutmeg
Crisp iceberg lettuce leaves
Light rye bread slices, lightly buttered

Blend salmon with celery, cucumber, eggs, and onion. In separate bowl, blend mayonnaise, lemon juice, mustard, dill weed, and nutmeg. Combine with salmon mixture and toss gently to blend well. Cover and chill. Place lettuce leaves on half of the bread slices and thickly spread the other half with the salmon mixture. Close sandwich and garnish with dill pickle fans.

Garnish:
Dill pickle fans*

Makes 8 to 10 sandwiches

*Comment: To add that special little touch, the dill pickle fans may be made by thinly slicing a whole pickle horizontally two-thirds the length of the pickle, then fan the slices open.

Hot Tuna and Egg Salad Sandwich

1 12½-ounce can tuna, drained and
   flaked
1 cup shredded Monterey Jack cheese
⅔ cup real mayonnaise
2 teaspoons fresh lemon juice
4 hard-cooked eggs, chopped
¼ cup chopped green pepper
¼ cup sliced green onion
3 tablespoons chopped sweet pickle
1½ teaspoons Dijon mustard
Salt and freshly ground pepper to taste
6 6-inch Italian rolls, split

Combine first 10 ingredients in large bowl. Spread mixture on rolls; close sandwiches and wrap individually in foil. Place on baking sheet; place in preheated 300°F oven until filling is hot, about 25 to 30 minutes.

Makes 6

Comment: This hot salad sandwich is great for a cold, wintry evening with a mug of tomato soup.

Dagwood Pork Sandwich

2 8-inch Italian rolls, sliced in
   half lengthwise
3 tablespoons butter or margarine,
   softened
1 pound lean ground pork
½ cup minced onion
1 clove garlic, minced
½ cup sliced celery
1 cup dairy sour cream
1 teaspoon dried dill weed
½ teaspoon salt
Few drops hot pepper sauce
2 firm tomatoes, sliced
1 green pepper, cut into thin rings
1 cup shredded mozzarella cheese

Spread rolls with 2 tablespoons butter or margarine; place each halved roll in 12-inch square of foil, folding edges up around the roll. Heat remaining 1 tablespoon butter or margarine in skillet. Sauté pork, onion, garlic, and celery until golden. Drain off fat. Add sour cream, dill weed, salt, and hot pepper sauce; taste for additional seasoning. Spread mixture on roll halves. Place slices of tomato and green pepper on top of meat and sprinkle with cheese. Do not close foil. Bake in preheated 375°F oven for 15 to 20 minutes, until heated through and cheese has melted.

Serves 4

Comment: Fold back the foil and use a knife and fork to eat these substantial sandwiches. Sweet pickle would complement the pork and mild cheese flavors.

Italian Open-Faced Fondue Sandwich

1 pound lean ground beef
1 clove garlic, minced
½ cup minced onion
1 15-ounce can tomato sauce
1 teaspoon dried oregano, crushed
½ teaspoon dried marjoram, crushed
½ teaspoon dried basil, crushed
3 cups shredded sharp Cheddar
   cheese
1½ cups shredded mozzarella cheese
1 tablespoon cornstarch
½ cup dry white wine or dry vermouth
8 slices ½-inch thick Italian bread,
   toasted
Chopped fresh parsley or cilantro*

In large heavy skillet, brown beef with garlic and onion; drain off fat. Add tomato sauce, herbs, Cheddar cheese, and 1 cup mozzarella cheese. Stir over low heat until the cheeses melt. Blend cornstarch and wine or vermouth together; stir into cheese mixture. Cook, stirring, until thick and bubbly. Spoon a portion of this topping over 2 slices toasted bread for each serving. Sprinkle top with remaining mozzarella cheese and parsley or cilantro.

*Cilantro is the parsley-like leaves of fresh coriander. It can be purchased in the specialty section of most supermarkets' produce departments.

Serves 4

Comment: Filling can be served in the traditional fondue pot and eaten with cubes of bread, but this open-faced sandwich is a nice change and convenient if you don't have a fondue pot. Add a crispy green salad with a vinaigrette dressing, candles, and a red tablecloth.

Mexican Steak Sandwich

1 pound lean sirloin or top round
½ teaspoon garlic powder
1 cup refried beans
½ cup grated sharp Cheddar cheese
3 tablespoons minced onion
1 tablespoon taco sauce
6 slices Italian bread, about ½-inch
   thick
2 tablespoons real butter, softened
Salt and freshly ground pepper to taste
1 avocado, thinly sliced
1 cup shredded iceberg lettuce
2 tomatoes, peeled and diced
Taco sauce

Have the butcher slice the meat or do it yourself by placing meat in freezer until firm but not frozen. Using sharp knife, trim and slice into ⅛-inch thick strips. Lightly sprinkle with garlic powder; let set at room temperature. Heat beans in small saucepan; mix in cheese, onion, and 1 tablespoon taco sauce. Butter bread slices and place on baking sheet. Spread each with refried bean mixture and lightly sprinkle with salt and pepper. Layer meat slices over beans. Broil 4 inches from heat for 5 minutes, watching carefully. Remove from oven and layer with slices of avocado, lettuce, and tomatoes. Pass taco sauce separately.

Serves 6

Comment: This full-meal supper sandwich needs only your favorite cold beverage to complete the meal.

Index

Born and raised in Topeka, Kansas, MIRIAM BAKER LOO is an accomplished and creative homemaker who has been an enthusiastic cook since her youth. After graduation from Washburn University of Topeka, Kansas, she was married to Orin Loo. In addition to raising three sons, with her husband in 1950 she founded Current, Inc., a national mail order firm located in Colorado Springs. The company has grown from a basement business, whose first product lines included Post-A-Notes and recipe cards designed by Mr. Loo, to a thriving enterprise serving millions of customers today.

A participant in many gourmet food classes, Miriam Loo has been responsible for all the recipes for notes, calendars, and personal enclosures in the Current line for several years.

Long involved in volunteer activities, Miriam Loo has received national recognition for accomplishments in community work, church leadership, and business.